THE END OF MARRIAGE

THE END
OF
MARRIAGE

David Morris

CASSELL · LONDON

CASSELL & COMPANY LTD
35 RED LION SQUARE, LONDON, WC1
Melbourne, Sydney, Toronto
Johannesburg, Auckland

First published 1971

I.S.B.N. 0 304 93695 2

Printed in Great Britain by
The Camelot Press Ltd,
London and Southampton
F. 1070

TO MY WIFE

who for over twenty years has devoted her energies to preserving our marriage while I have spent mine on ending the marriages of others less fortunate than myself.

I ———— take thee ———— to my wedded (wife) (husband) to have and to hold from this day forward, for better for worse, for richer for poorer, in sickness and in health, to love and to cherish, till death us do part, according to God's holy ordinance; and thereto I plight thee my troth.

From the Form of Solemnization of Matrimony in the Book of Common Prayer the use of which was enjoined by the Act of Uniformity 1559 in the reign of Elizabeth I.

Divorce by consent after two years' separation and divorce against the will of the deserted spouse after five years' separation were introduced by the Divorce Reform Act 1969 in the reign of Elizabeth II.

FOREWORD

This is an unusual book. It is a plain man's guide to marriage law written by a lawyer. Now lawyers, unless they are asked to edit a new edition of *Rayden on Divorce* or one of the other well-known legal textbooks, seldom write about marriage and divorce, and when they edit such a textbook they are seldom concerned to canvass the plain man's opinions.

In a sense this is a pity, because ordinarily an experienced lawyer knows the inside story of many marriages, particularly if he is a solicitor. David Morris was my pupil shortly after he was called to the Bar, and is now a solicitor of many years' standing which enables him to write with the authority of an unusually wide experience.

His conclusion is paradoxical. But, as it is a paradox I largely share myself, I hope it will be widely studied, and, if not accepted, at least not rejected for inadequate reasons.

'One major theme emerges,' he writes, 'the slow and still uncompleted improvement in the wife's legal position. . . . It all sounds wonderful until you face the position of the middle-aged woman with young children abandoned by her husband for a younger woman after ten or fifteen years of marriage. Then by a paradox many of those improvements, to which in all fairness women were clearly entitled, seem to have contributed to a weakening of women's position in marriage as a whole.'

What he means by this paradox, David Morris makes clear in the course of his book, which tells the story of the divorce law from medieval times to the latest Act passed in the present Parliament. He is no friend of the 'breakdown of the marriage' theory of divorce made popular by recent commissions and now embodied, theoretically, at least, in the new Act. The matrimonial offence, he considers, is very much alive.

'I agree,' he writes, 'that there are often faults on both sides, but I believe that in many cases if all the facts were known most people would say that far more of the fault was on one side than the other.' That, too, has been my experience.

Mr. Morris believes in divorce by consent, about which I am a little more sceptical. But, like me, he considers the provision in the new Act for divorce at the suit of the 'guilty' party after five years is a prescription for bringing about injustice. 'One hundred and twelve years after divorce first became available in a court of law, women's well-justified struggle for equality has now ended in a situation where a divorce can be forced on an innocent wife against her will after years of marriage. A well-meaning attempt to help illegitimate children has put the young mistress in a stronger position than the old wife. . . . It is an odd end to an odd story. . . . I cannot help thinking that the champions of women's rights have been asleep during the past few years and will awake to find that the male has won the last battle in a hundred years' war.'

David Morris's experience of matrimonial litigation is now so much greater than my own that he writes with far greater authority than I can now hope to summon. But I am bound to say that my own experience, such as it is, has led me to the same melancholy conclusion.

It seems to me that social and ecclesiastical writers on divorce, and members of Parliament and peers who discuss it in Parliament, approach the subject from too theoretical and academic a viewpoint. Apart from theological questions which I am not really qualified to discuss, divorce law (where it does not reflect disputes about the care and maintenance of children) is about economics. Divorce is not so much the end of one marriage, as a licence to contract another. Can a man afford two households, where one of the wives is unable to work either because she has to look after the children, or because after years of marriage her earning capacity has been diminished? No doubt, when the second wife, who is in possession, works too, the situation is less acute. But it remains difficult. And it is really not good enough to appeal to principles of sex equality. Women may be equal to men as human beings, but they are infinitely more vulnerable, and law which does not take account of this fact is out of touch with the realities of life. Moreover third, or even fourth marriages have now become sufficiently frequent not to be wholly disregarded by the legislator. If a man can afford two wives, how is he placed with three or four? Supplementary benefit is sometimes rather cold comfort for a deserted wife with young children to bring up and a maintenance order which she cannot enforce against a husband who has no intention of obeying it.

I wish David Morris's book every success. It is well, wittily, and compassionately written. Of course, lawyers often over-simplify their experience, and, like others, generalize too readily from it. Also we tend to look on the seamy side. Most of us have known the story of many unhappy marriages. Of happy marriages the luckiest of us have known the inner story of only one, our own. But there are few who will not gain insight into the subject by reading this book. Whether or not they agree with its conclusion they will be better qualified to form their own opinions on the subject after they have read it.

Quintin Hogg
April 1970

CONTENTS

CONTENTS

ACKNOWLEDGEMENTS

I am grateful to the President of the Probate Divorce and Admiralty Division of the Supreme Court, Sir Jocelyn Simon, for permission to quote from three of his speeches; to Sir John Compton Miller, the Senior Registrar of the Divorce Registry, for permission to inspect some of the older Court records and to publish pleadings, some, as in the Parnell case, for the first time; to Mr. W. I. Martyn of the Divorce Registry, to Mr. Maurice Bond, Clerk of the Records at the Record Office, House of Lords, and to Mr. A. Derby, Librarian to the Law Society, for their help. In my account of Legal Aid I have very kindly been allowed to make use of a series of articles by Mr. C. F. Wegg-Prosser, Solicitor of the Supreme Court, and I have also been helped by Mr. Seton Pollock, Solicitor of the Supreme Court, Secretary at the Law Society responsible for Legal Aid.

My friends Mr. Mark Smith, M.A.(Cantab.) of the Middle Temple, Barrister-at-Law, and Sir Arthur Driver, J.P., Solicitor of the Supreme Court, have been good enough to read the book in typescript and to make some helpful suggestions.

My former Master at the Bar, the Right Honourable Quintin Hogg, P.C., Q.C., M.P., has taken the time out of an incredibly busy life to write a foreword.

Mr. Nicholas Merriman of the Inner Temple, Barrister-at-Law, Miss S. Freeman, B.A., LL.B.(Rand), Attorney of the Supreme Court of South Africa, and my wife, a graduate of London University, have helped me in gathering some of the material used in work on this book.

To all these I am deeply grateful. No one except myself is responsible for the sometimes contentious views expressed. It hardly seems possible to write about divorce without being contentious.

For permission to quote or make use of material from the books, newspapers, periodicals and documents set out below I sincerely thank the following:

Butterworth from *Rayden on Divorce* (First, Third, Fourth

and Fifth Editions), Halsbury's *Laws of England* (Third Edition) and *The Formation and Annulment of Marriage* (Second Edition) by Joseph Jackson, Q.C., LL.B.(Cantab.), LL.M. (Lond.); the Clarendon Press from *The Age of Reform 1815–1870* by E. L. Woodward, *England 1870–1914* by R. C. K. Ensor, *English History 1914–1945* by A. J. P. Taylor which are all part of the Oxford History of England and also *Victorian England—The Portrait of An Age* by G. M. Young; Ernest Benn Ltd. and the estate of H. G. Wells from *Divorce as I See It*; George Allen and Unwin Ltd. from Volume II of Bertrand Russell's *Autobiography*; Geoffrey Bles Ltd. from *The Screwtape Letters* by C. S. Lewis, first published in 1942; Sir Alan Herbert, C.H. (to whom I have referred throughout as A. P. Herbert), from *Holy Deadlock*; Her Majesty's Stationery Office from *Hansard* and the Reports of Royal Commissions; The Incorporated Council of Law Reporting for England and Wales from the *Law Reports* and *Weekly Law Reports*; Macmillan and the estate of Thomas Hardy from *Jude the Obscure*; the *New Statesman* and Mr. Alan Brien from an article by him; Penguin Books Ltd. and Mr. Ronald Fletcher from his book *Britain in the Sixties—The Family and Marriage*; the Clerk of the Records, Record Office, House of Lords in respect of the Bill of Lord Roos, the Petition of Lady Roos and William Miller's Petition of 1821; the Society of Authors and the Estate of Bernard Shaw from the Preface to *Getting Married*; the *Solicitors' Journal* from articles by C. F. Wegg-Prosser and the author; the *Spectator* from a comment on the Mordaunt case; Stevens & Sons Ltd. and Mr. Justice Megarry for quotations from *A Manual of the Law of Real Property* and *Miscellany at Law*; *The Times*; William Heinemann Ltd. from *The Forsyte Saga* by John Galsworthy; Victor Gollancz from *The Reform of the Law* and *Law Reform Now*; Heineman Educational Books Ltd. from *Divorce in England* by O. R. McGregor; Modern Law Review Limited from an article by C. P. Harvey, Q.C.

All Parliamentary speeches are quoted from *Hansard*. In this book I give some actual pleadings from cases and some fictitious examples. The forms of the latter are taken from the precedents to *Rayden on Divorce* in the Editions referred to above.

May 1970

INTRODUCTION

There is no subject on which more dangerous nonsense is taught and thought than marriage. . . . Speaking for myself, I can say that I know the inside history of perhaps half a dozen marriages. Any family Solicitor knows more than this; but even a family Solicitor, however large his practice, knows nothing of the million households which have no solicitors, and which nevertheless make marriage what it really is.

GEORGE BERNARD SHAW: From the Preface to *Getting Married*
(1908)

I'm trying to make you study the chart before you put to sea. You've no idea what rocks are ahead. Few people have. For the poor devils who do make the passage keep quiet about it. You're all the same. You prance into my office and ask me to get you a divorce as you'd ask me to get you a dog licence; and sooner or later you all open your innocent eyes and say 'I'd no idea that it was all so difficult'.

A. P. HERBERT: *Holy Deadlock* (1934)

In 1929 I published 'Marriage and Morals'. . . . In it I developed the view that complete fidelity was not to be expected in most marriages, but that a husband and wife ought to be able to remain good friends in spite of affairs. I did not maintain, however, that a marriage could with advantage be prolonged if the wife had a child or children of whom the husband was not the father; in that case, I thought, divorce was desirable. I do not know what I think now about the subject of marriage. There seem to be insuperable objections to every general theory about it. Perhaps easy divorce causes less unhappiness than any other system, but I am no longer capable of being dogmatic on the subject of marriage.

BERTRAND RUSSELL: *The Autobiography of Bertrand Russell*
Vol. II (1968)

Of all actions of a man's life his marriage does least concern other people, yet of all actions of our life 'tis most meddled with by other people. Marriage is nothing but a civil contract. 'Tis true, 'tis an ordinance of God: so is every other contract; God commands me to keep it when I have made it.

JOHN SELDEN: *Table Talk* (1689)

This book is part history, part guide to divorce law—now and in the near future—and part a means of working off my own views and prejudices formed from twenty years' experience of divorce work, first as a barrister and later as a solicitor. For a long time I have wanted to step back from the day to day rush and see how it all developed. I hope it will be of some interest, and possibly help, to those who are facing the breakdown of their marriage and who contemplate with well justified horror the sometimes squalid, often difficult and nearly always sad process of ending matters. It deals with the unhappy position of children of divided homes and looks at the maze of law relating to property rights. It shows the changing attitude of society at large as reflected in Acts of Parliament and the changing attitude of the Courts as reflected in law reports. It is a story of the gradual extension of the grounds of divorce and of the gradual increase of the availability of divorce. From the divorce by Private Act of Parliament in the eighteenth century for the very few and very rich to the undefended divorce in a County Court now for the many, a great number of whom receive financial assistance from the State to enable them to bring proceedings, the story reflects the whole social history of England and Wales. One major theme emerges—the slow and still uncompleted improvement in the wife's legal position. The grounds on which she may ask for a divorce, her rights to custody of the children and her property rights have all changed in her favour. Independently of the law of divorce women's position has improved generally by increased political rights, increased education, increased financial independence and increased ability to control the consequences of sexual intercourse. It all sounds wonderful until you face the position of the middle-aged woman with young children abandoned by her husband for a younger woman after ten or fifteen years of marriage. Then by a paradox many of those improvements, to which in all fairness women were clearly entitled, seem to have contributed to a weakening of women's position in marriage as a whole. It is a paradox which I hope to make clear by the end of this book.

One of the leading legal textbooks on divorce is already over 2,500 pages long. There are many important aspects of matrimonial law which I have not dealt with at all or have barely touched on such as domicil, the recognition of foreign divorce decrees, insanity, decrees of presumption of death, declarations of legitimacy, the modern law of nullity and judicial separation. I do not refer to the thousands of cases dealt with in Magistrates' Courts. I have attempted to describe only the major steps in the history of divorce in this country and to discuss only those topics which have most commonly affected those who become involved in divorce proceedings.

The method I have used is to show how a person who wanted to end his marriage went about it at various significant dates, the grounds which were available, the form of procedure which had to be used and the resulting position of the children and of property rights.

Where I refer to 'the Church' I mean the Western as opposed to the Eastern Church. The latter has taken a much less rigid view on divorce than the former.

I did not set out in life with the intention or in the expectation of spending most of my working days in divorce work. Although inevitably it has more sorrow and strain in it than other aspects of the law I do not regret the way things have turned out. In the words of Lord Denning over twenty years ago:

No branch of the law is more important than that which relates to divorce. It has a profound effect on family life which is the foundation of society.

Lastly, I hope that no critic will be as severe on me as Milton was on the anonymous opponent of his *Doctrine and Discipline of Divorce* of whom he said:

His instances out of the common law are all so quite beside the matter which he would prove, as may be a warning to all clients how they venture their business with such a cockbrained solicitor.

1

THE END OF MARRIAGE BEFORE 1550—
DEATH OR NULLITY

Indissoluble marriage is an academic figment, advocated only by celibates and by comfortably married people who imagine that if other couples are unfortunate it must be their own fault, just as rich people are apt to imagine that if other people are poor it serves them right. There is always some means of dissolution.
GEORGE BERNARD SHAW: From the Preface to *Getting Married* (1908)

It does not appear manifest at what time [Henry VIII's] scruples began nor whether they preceded his passion for Anne Boleyn . . . there can be little doubt that weariness of Catherine's person, a woman considerably older than himself, and unlikely to bear more children, had a far greater effect on his conscience than the study of Thomas Aquinas or any other theologian. It by no means follows from hence that, according to the casuistry of the Catholic church and the principles of the Canon law, the merits of that famous process were so much against Henry, as, out of dislike to him and pity for his queen, we are apt to imagine, and as the writers of that persuasion have subsequently assumed.
HENRY HALLAM: *The Constitutional History of England* (1827)

Divorce by mutual consent was allowed under Roman law and in the seventh century in England the *Penitentials* of Theodore declared marriages dissoluble either by mutual consent, or for adultery, desertion, impotence, relationship, long absence and captivity. Gradually, however, the Church's doctrine of lifelong monogamy prevailed. It was better to marry than to burn, but if you got married you were stuck with your partner. Marriage could only be ended in a way which made remarriage possible by death or a decree of nullity. However, as most people died much younger most marriages did not last as long as they do today. For some at least of the tougher few who survived, death provided the opportunity for a succession of marriage partners. In the Prologue to the *Canterbury Tales*, Chaucer tells us that the Wife of Bath was 'a worthy woman all her life' despite the fact that she indulged in premarital sexual intercourse. At the time of her pilgrimage to the Holy Shrine at Canterbury she had worn out and out-lived five husbands and was eagerly looking forward to her sixth:

> Welcome the sixte whan that evere he shal,
> For sinth I wol nat keepe me chast in al,
> Whan myn housbande is fro the world agoon,
> Som Cristen man shal wedde me anoon.

Even during the Victorian period when contemporary morality regarded divorce as an abomination, death often relieved many a Victorian father from the task of remaining faithful to his wife after she had lost her sexual attraction by excessive child-bearing. Indeed by the very process of getting his wife with child too frequently he might contribute to her early death and after a socially acceptable period of heavy mourning—comparable to the enforced period of waiting today between decree nisi and decree absolute in a divorce suit—he might be able to find a younger and more attractive helpmeet in the governess hired to teach his first brood.

For those husbands or wives who found their spouses impossible to live with but in good health the alternative remedy was to obtain a decree of nullity in the Ecclesiastical Courts. The Church was unwilling to sanction divorce so as to enable re-marriage. It would only permit decrees equivalent to a present-day decree of judicial separation which relieved the spouses of their matrimonial obligations although they remained married. These were decrees of separation *a mensa et thoro* (i.e. from bed and board) as distinct from decrees *a vinculo matrimonii* (from the bonds of marriage) which permitted remarriage. However, for the really determined there was an escape route. The Church was unwilling to end a marriage. It was willing to say that a marriage had never begun. In the words of the Book of Common Prayer—'Those whom God hath joined together let no man put asunder.' But curiously enough it was permissible to say that God should never have joined them together in the

5

first place. No matter how long the marriage had lasted or how many children had been born, if it could be proved that on some ground the marriage was initially invalid, it was declared never to have existed and the parties were free to marry someone else.

Considerable ingenuity was employed in finding technical flaws which could be exploited to obtain a decree of nullity.

Two main lines of attack were used, the first directed against the ceremony of marriage and the second using impediments to marriage. The Church's doctrine with regard to ceremonies of marriage may seem strange but it started from the premise that sexual intercourse outside marriage was a sin and went on from there to conclude that any cloak which could be wrapped round the naked fact of sexual intercourse was better than none. It was not anxious, therefore, to make the requirements for a valid ceremony too strict; it preferred a looser definition which could cover an ambiguous situation with the Church's blessing. But if the requirements for a valid marriage ceremony are not clearly defined, some day an unhappily married person will consult his or her lawyer and together they will start to wonder whether there is any possibility of planning a way out.

By Henry VIII's time this was a popular method of ending marriage. An Act of 1540 referred to many persons whose marriages were in doubt and an Act of 1548 spoke of:

> Women and men breaking their own promises and faiths made by the one unto the other, so set upon sensuality and pleasure, that if after the contract of matrimony they might have whom they more favoured and desired, they could be content by lightness of nature to overturn all that they had done before.

As to impediments, Joseph Jackson writes:

> But while the church treated marriage as a formless contract which could be arrived at by words of present consent alone, the church, somewhat reckless of the consequences, illogically multiplied impediments to valid marriages, making the formation of an unimpeachable marriage something of a matter of chance.

Amongst impediments the twin blessings were consanguinity, i.e. relationship by blood, and affinity, i.e. relationship through marriage. The prohibited degrees were extensive and affinity came into the picture because the Church taught that sexual union made man and woman one flesh. Joseph Jackson says of the law of affinity that it was: 'extremely complex: it was a mixture of mathematics and mysticism'. As I am neither a mathematician nor a mystic I do not propose to attempt an exposition of the law. We need only be concerned with the consequences. They are set out in the following passage from the Report of the Royal Commission in 1853:

> Every one knows how much it was the policy of the Roman Church to multiply impediments to matrimony; the power of granting dispensations having been in all ages a fruitful source of Ecclesiastical revenue. Not only were marriages with cousins interdicted, but the relation of affinity was held to be contracted by mere commerce between the sexes. Thus, if a man had carnally known one sister, though not married to her, it would have been incestuous in him to marry, or to have sexual intercourse with the other sister, or even with her relatives, by consanguinity or affinity, to the eighth degree! Thus, on the death of James IV. of Scotland, his widow Margaret Tudor married the Earl of Angus. In 1524 she procured (by collusion with her husband) a sentence of Divorce ā vinculo matrimonii upon proof of his having been 'precontracted'. Sentence of nullity (that is, in the Ecclesiastical phraseology, Divorce ā vinculo matrimonii) was thereupon pronounced; and the Queen, freed from her fetters, gave her hand to Lord Methven, whom however, she very soon dismissed by another suit in the Ecclesiastical Court, upon evidence that Methven was cousin, eight degrees removed, to her former husband, Angus; this constituting an affinity by the laws of holy Church, and a just impediment to matrimony. In another case, Janet Betoun [the Lady Buccleugh of the *Lay of the Last Minstrel*], having married Simon Preston of Craigmillar, sued a Divorce against him in the Ecclesiastical Court, not on the ground of any misconduct on his part, but on the ground that before their marriage she, the plaintiff, had had sinful intercourse with Walter Scott, of Buccleugh, and that Buccleugh and Preston were within the prohibited degrees. On proof of these allegations, a sentence of Divorce ā vinculo matrimonii was pronounced. These cases are set out in Mr. Riddell's 'Exposition of Ancient Consistorial Law', published at Edinburgh, in 1842. They show most clearly what the law was in the Roman Catholic times on the points in question. . . . It is not to be supposed that the English Ecclesiastical law was less liberal or less accommodating than that of Scotland; for Lord Coke tells, that there was a time in

England when Divorce ā vinculo matrimonii might be had because the husband had stood godfather to his wife's cousin. It was not by the axe that Henry VIII extinguished his marriage with Anne Boleyn. He first carried her into the Ecclesiastical Court, and got a sentence against her, for an alleged precontract with Northumberland, and for his own criminal intercourse with her sister Mary. In the Roman Catholic times, the same Ecclesiastical law prevailed throughout the island, and, indeed, governed the entire Christian world.

By Henry VIII's time things had reached such a pitch that in the preamble to the Act of 1540 it was stated:

> Marriages have been brought into such an uncertainty thereby that no marriage could be so surely knit or bounden but it should lie in either of the parties power to prove a precontract, a kindred and alliance, or a carnal knowledge to defeat the same—

as none knew better than the King when he gave his royal assent.

Latimer, in his last sermon before Edward VI, is reported to have urged the King:

> to take an order for marriages here in England. For here is marriage for pleasure, and voluptuousness, and for goods: and so that they may join land to land, and possessions to possessions: they care for no more here in England. And that is the cause of so much adultery, and so much breach of wedlock in the noblemen and gentlemen, and so much divorcing. And it is not now in the noblemen only, but it is come to the inferior sort. Every man, if he have but a small cause, will cast off his old wife, and take a new, and will marry again at his pleasure: and there be many that have so done. I would therefore wish that there were a law provided in this behalf for adulterers, and that adultery should be punished, and that might be a remedy for all this matter.

For a second offence of adultery he advocated punishment by death. In his book *The Formation and Annulment of Marriage*, Jackson writes:

> In 1554 Archbishop Hamilton reported to the Pope that it was hardly possible for men and women of good families to find partners that they were qualified to marry: some nevertheless contracted marriage, promising to obtain a dispensation, but this might take two or three years during which time the parties might choose to have the marriage annulled, thus bastardising their children.

Today a petitioner must normally wait for three years after the marriage before presenting a Petition for divorce. In pre-Reformation times with a much smaller and less mobile population, where in most villages as well as in 'good families' there must have been a considerable degree of inter-relationship it would probably have been possible for a considerably greater number to have had their marriages annulled if they had had the knowledge and means to start proceedings. On the other hand, whilst the Church was prepared to tolerate a situation where the 'good families' could get out of the matrimonial bond if they chose to do so, the rules might have been tightened up considerably if the 'inferior sort' had started to follow in large numbers the example of the 'good families'.

To obtain a decree of nullity the unhappy spouse had to go to the Ecclesiastical Courts. The separation of Ecclesiastical and Civil Courts began at the time of William the Conqueror. Eventually the Church Courts had criminal jurisdiction in respect of all offences of the clergy and of churchwardens in connection with their office, heresy, brawling in church or churchyard and defamation. Their civil jurisdiction included probate of wills and grants of administration and all matrimonial causes.

The Courts of first instance were the Diocesan or Consistory Courts. There were twenty-two in the province of Canterbury and four in the province of York. Appeals could be brought from the Consistory Courts to the Court of Arches in the province of Canterbury and to the Court of Chancery in the province of York. These Courts still function. Until Henry VIII's reign a further appeal could be taken to Rome; later, appeals could be brought to the Judicial Committee of the Privy Council, but instead of being concerned as they might have been in Henry VIII's time with whether or not to grant the King a divorce or decree of nullity they were likely to deal with such matters as a struggle by a dwindling band of loyal parishioners to prevent the amalgamation of their almost empty church with another equally empty church not far away.

The Church Courts dealt with decrees of separation from bed and board in cases of adultery, cruelty and unnatural offences and decrees of nullity in cases of consanguinity or affinity, mental incapacity, impotence, force or error, non-age or a prior existing marriage. A suit of jactitation of marriage could be brought to prevent a person falsely boasting that he or she was married to another. The Church also dealt with desertion and did so in a way which was to have important results for the law of divorce between 1884 and 1923. By a decree for restitution of conjugal rights the Court ordered the deserting spouse to return. Disobedience resulted in excommunication, until 1813 when imprisonment for not more than six months was substituted for excommunication.

Writing in 1849, John MacQueen, who was Secretary to the Royal Commission of 1850, summed up the position as follows:

> In fact, parties who sighed for their liberty did not often, in those days, sigh in vain; for wherever a marriage became hateful to one or other or both, of the spouses, the canonists rarely failed to demonstrate that it was invalid; the only proof required by the Court being the mere confession of the parties. . . . Thus, in cases of adultery, the injured party had no more stringent remedy than divorce a mensa et thoro—a sort of insult rather than a satisfaction to any man of ordinary feelings and understanding. But if by the fertile exercise of canonical ingenuity some ante-nuptial disability could be suggested, complete redress would be given; for the contract would be pronounced invalid, and both parties would then have their freedom. The labours of the canonists, therefore, in this department, ought not to be the subject of indiscriminating censure, since by means of them, the community was in a great degree relieved from the severe and unbearable consequences which would otherwise have sprung from an undeviating adherence to the iron doctrine of indissolubility.

2

DIVORCE FOR THE VERY FEW AND VERY RICH—THE EIGHTEENTH CENTURY

One of the consequences of basing marriage on the considerations stated with cold abhorrence by Saint Paul . . . is that the sex slavery involved has become complicated by economic slavery; so that whilst the man defends marriage because he is really defending his pleasures, the woman is even more vehement on the same side because she is defending her only means of livelihood. To a woman without property or marketable talent a husband is more necessary than a master to a dog.
GEORGE BERNARD SHAW: From the Preface to *Getting Married*
(1908)

As for what they say we must bear with patience, to bear with patience, and to seek effectuall remedies, implies no contradiction. It may no lesse be for our disobedience, our unfaithfulnes, and other sins against God, that wives becom adulterous to the bed, and questionles we ought to take the affliction as patiently, as christian prudence would wish; yet hereby is not lost the right of divorcing for adultery. No you say, because our Saviour excepted that only. But why, if he were so bent to punish our sins, and try our patience in binding on us a disastrous mariage, why did he except adultery? Certainly to have bin bound from divorce in that case also had bin as plentifull a punishment to our sins, and not too little work for the patientest. Nay perhaps they will say it was too great a sufferance: And with as slight a reason, for no wise man but would sooner pardon the act of adultery once and again committed by a person worth pitty and forgivnes, than to lead a wearisom life of unloving & unquiet conversation with one who neither affects nor is affected, much lesse with one who exercises all bitternes, and would commit adultery too, but for envy lest the persecuted condition should thereby get the benefit of his freedom. 'Tis plain therefore that God enjoyns not this supposed strictnes of not divorcing either to punish us, or to try our patience.
JOHN MILTON: *Tetrachordon* (1644)

Towards the end of Henry VIII's reign it seemed possible for a time that divorce might then be introduced into English law. A statute was passed in 1533–34 granting the King authority to nominate persons to examine ecclesiastical law and in Edward VI's reign a similar statute was passed as a result of which in 1551 a Commission was issued to the Archbishop of Canterbury and others. A draft code was prepared by Cranmer and published under the title of *Reformatio Legum Ecclesiasticarum*. It contemplated divorce on the grounds of adultery, contumacious desertion after two or three years, deadly hostility, persistent cruelty, and too long absence without news of the absentee. The innocent party was to have the right to re-marry; separations *a mensa et thoro* were to be abolished; the Ecclesiastical Courts were to retain jurisdiction in divorce; the guilty party was subject to the punishment of either perpetual banishment or imprisonment for life. Fornication was to be punished by penance and (if necessary) excommunication and by a penalty of £10 (or as much as could be conveniently spared) to be placed in the poor box.

The code never became law but in Scotland from the end of the sixteenth century onwards divorce was allowed for adultery and desertion and no distinction was made between husband and wife as to the grounds on which a divorce might be obtained.

The position in England from 1550 to the end of the century is not absolutely certain but it now seems accepted that after a case decided in the Court of Star Chamber in 1601 it was not possible for a valid English marriage to be dissolved by judicial process. In view of the fact that the bounds of consanguinity and affinity as grounds for decrees of nullity were restricted in England at the time of the Reformation it was therefore more difficult to end a marriage in England after 1601 than it had ever been before. In the words of the Report of the Royal Commission in 1853:

> The doctrine of indissolubility was thus not only re-established, but it operated in this country with a rigour unknown in Roman Catholic times; the various fictions and devices in the shape of canonical degrees and alleged precontracts, which then afforded so many loopholes of escape from its severity, having been each and all put an end to at the Reformation.

However, not everyone was content with their married state and amongst those whose marital disharmony prompted thought on the subject of ending marriage was John Milton. He approached the subject from a lofty, religious, and exclusively male point of view and made his plea for divorce on the grounds that a more perfect spiritual union could justify divorce and remarriage. Writing in *Tetrachordon* in 1644 of Verse 27 from the first Chapter of Genesis, Milton said:

So God created man in his own image, in the image of God created he him; male and female created he them.

Not but that particular exceptions may have place if she exceed her husband in prudence and dexterity, and he contentedly yield, for then a superior and more naturall law comes in that the wiser should govern the lesse wise, whether male or female. But that which far more easily and obediently follows from this verse, is that, seeing that woman was purposely made for man, and he her head, it cannot stand before the breath of this divine utterance that man the portraiture of God, joyning to himself for his intended good and solace an inferiour sexe, should so become her thrall, whose wilfulness or inability to be a wife frustrates the occasional end of her creation, but that he may acquitt himself to freedom by his naturall birthright, and that indeleble character of priority which God crown'd him with. If it be urged that sin hath lost him this, the answer is not far to seek, that from her the sin first proceeded, which keeps her justly in the same proportion still beneath.

He argued that there were more important grounds than adultery for divorce and in his work *The Doctrine and Discipline of Divorce* said:

God regards love and peace in the family more than a compulsive performance of marriage which is more broken by a grievous continuance, than by a needful divorce . . . sometimes continuance in marriage may be evidently the shortening and endangering of life to either party, both law and divinity concluding that life is to be preferred before marriage, the intended solace of life. It is probable or rather certain that everyone who happens to marry, hath not the calling, and therefore upon unfitness found and considered, force ought not to be used . . . marriage is not a mere carnal coition but a humane society: where that cannot reasonably be had there can be no true matrimony.

Milton was not long left unanswered. In a pamphlet *An Answer to a Book Intituled the Doctrine and Discipline of Divorce or a Plea for Ladies and Gentlewomen and all other married women against Divorce*, the writer rejected Milton's arguments based on Biblical texts and argued that if divorce were allowed, quarrels and discontents would be manufactured deliberately. The writer went on:

> Who sees not how many thousands of lustful and libidinous men would be parting from their wives every week and marrying others; and upon this, who should keep the children of these divorcers which sometimes they would leave in their wives bellies?

He went on to refer to:

> the overturning and overthrowing of all humane society which would inevitably follow if this loose doctrine of divorce were once established by law.

The arguments set out above for and against divorce were much the same arguments that have taken place ever since when any change in the law relating to divorce has been contemplated.

For Milton there was no divorce, but death twice permitted him to remarry. Apart from death or nullity there gradually developed a third method of ending marriage. This was important, not so much because of the principle or numbers involved, but because, in the period of reform in the 1830s, it came to be thought that what had been a privilege for the few should be extended to others. The method was to procure the passing of a Private Act of Parliament. The supremacy of Parliament had been achieved and by Public or Private Act, Parliament could enact that in law black was white and in the Courts black would subsequently be held to be white, although an occasional courageous or obstinate judge might hold that Parliament had really only intended to make black grey. By the general law of the country in the eighteenth century there could be no divorce. But exceptions to the general law could be and were made by Private Act of Parliament. In March 1771 a Bill was passed by the House of Lords:

> to prevent any Bill from being brought into Parliament for the Dissolution of any Marriage for the cause of adultery, unless a

clause or particular words be inserted, to prevent the Person against whom the Adultery has been proved from marrying or contracting Matrimony with the Person with whom he or she shall be proved to have carried on such criminal Intercourse; and to declare the Issue of such marriage incapable of inheriting.

The Bill was rejected by the House of Commons where the proceedings were reported as follows (the italics are mine):

The arguments in favour of the Bill were, that this Bill would in some degree check the frequent adulteries, as no lady could rely on the promises of a lover to marry her in case of a divorce: that it would put a lady on her guard against a false friend, who, under the cloak of friendship, might insinuate himself into the family, and taking part in the quarrels of man and wife, take advantage of little opportunities to prevail over the lady's virtue: *that the facility with which divorces were now obtained,* made it to be feared, that forgiving people would on false suggestions, and bare proofs, apply for them, when there was no other cause but dislike in the parties, and that, in some measure, this would throw a damp on such applications.

Mr Burke did in a very ingenious manner, urge several motives for passing the Bill. Lords Beauchamp and Strange, and Mr. Fox, opposed the Bill. It was urged that this would by no means stop the frequency of adulteries, as the prospect of a future marriage was too distant a temptation to the commitment of it, the present passions being evidently the cause: that it was levelled against the ladies, and would leave those who were so unfortunate as to be seduced in the worst situation possible, in so bad a one, that declaring she should not marry the person she had sinned with, it must either follow, that she would cohabit with him, to the scandal of society, or else must be debarred society, and be deemed improper to marry at all, as none else would probably marry her: that the principle of the Bill, if extended, would be of the utmost detriment to population, *as few marriages were contracted among the poor people but by the man to the girl he had debauched*: that the Bill was also ridiculous in itself, since it bound the legislature to a rule, which every subsequent act of divorce might repeal, or confirm, as parliament pleased, and which rule might be followed by the insertion of this clause, without a formal act of parliament.

'Few marriages were contracted among the poor people but by the man to the girl he had debauched'—apparently pre-marital intercourse is not a wholly novel feature of recent years.

'*The facility with which divorces were now obtained*'—at the time
when the Bill was being debated the number of divorces by
Private Act of Parliament was about one a year. The Royal
Commission of 1909–12 said that from the end of the seven-
teenth century 'Acts of Parliament dissolving marriage became
frequent'. The Commissioners appointed to inquire into the law
of divorce in 1850 reported as follows:

> At first only a few Divorce Bills were passed—not more than
> five were carried through Parliament before the accession of the
> House of Hanover. From 1715 to 1775 their number was sixty,
> that is to say, they averaged about one a year. From 1775 to 1780
> they had increased to seventy-four, that is to say, upon an average,
> to about three a year: and from 1800 to 1852, they amounted to
> one hundred and ten.

In all between 1700 and 1857 there were about two hundred
and thirty divorces by Private Act of Parliament of which four
only were obtained by women. In 1968 there were 45,036
decrees absolute of divorce and 758 decrees of nullity. Between
1801 and 1968 the population of England and Wales rose from
approximately 8,892,000 to 48,593,000.

The process by Private Act of Parliament was open to all
provided they had position and influence, considerable wealth,
persistence and in some cases, sufficient lack of scruples. If it
seems quite outrageous that wealth could buy a privilege
denied to almost all, we must remember that even in the
second half of the nineteenth century when the law was
theoretically the same for all, the cost of obtaining a divorce
put it out of reach for most people. In the familiar saying, the
Law Courts were then open to all—like the Ritz Hotel.

The first occasion after 1601 when a Private Bill was passed
by Parliament to enable a husband to remarry was in 1670.
The case was that of Lord Roos (or Ross), later Earl of Rutland. Having obtained a decree in the Ecclesiastical Courts on
the grounds of his wife's adultery, Lord Roos promoted a Bill
in Parliament on 5 March 1667. (Appendix A sets out the
Petition of Lady Anne Roos in opposition to her husband's
Bill.) It did not receive the Royal Assent until 10 April 1670,
and it did not have an easy passage through Parliament. All
the Roman Catholic peers and nearly all the bishops voted
against it. The debate on the first Reading lasted till ten

o'clock at night and the Bill only got through on the second Reading by a few votes. Amongst those who followed the debates in the House of Lords was Charles II himself who is said to have declared that 'it was better than going to a play', a feeling he seems to have shared with those members of the public who have since crowded into Court rooms during well-publicized divorce cases.

But why was Charles II there and why was Lord Roos the first person to get a Private Bill through, thereby starting a train of events which gradually but perhaps inevitably led to the thousands of undefended divorces today? So far as Lord Roos was concerned the main object of the Bill was not so much to enable him to remarry as by so doing to have legitimate children with the capacity of inheriting. This is made clear by the Act itself which is in the following terms:

An Act for John Manners, called Lord Roos, to marry again. For as much as John Manners, commonly called Lord Roos, only son and heir apparent of John, Earl of Rutland, being formerly married to the Lady Ann Pierpoint, is, by sentence of the Ecclesiastical Court, justly divorced from her for adultery on her part; and her children, by Act of this present Parliament, have been declared illegitimate, and no probable expectation of posterity to support the family in the male line but by the said John Manners Lord Roos: the King's most excellent Majesty therefore, upon the humble petitions of the said John Earl of Rutland and the said John Manners, called Lord Roos, and others their relations, and for other weighty considerations, is pleased that it be enacted, and be it enacted, by the King's most excellent Majesty, with the advice and consent of the Lords Spiritual and Temporal, and Commons, in this present Parliament assembled, and by the authority of the same, That it shall, and may be lawful to and for the said John Manners, called Lord Roos, at any time or times hereafter, to contract matrimony, and to marry as well in the lifetime of the said Lady Ann as if she were naturally dead, with any other woman or women with whom he might lawfully marry in case the said Lady Ann was not living; and that such matrimony, when had and celebrated, shall be good, just, and lawful, and so shall be adjudged, deemed and taken to all intents, constructions, and purposes, and that all and every children and child born in such matrimony shall be deemed, adjudged, and taken to be born in lawful wedlock, and to be legitimate and inheritable, and shall inherit the said earldom of Rutland, and all other dignities, baronies, honours, and titles of houses, lands, tenements, and other hereditaments from and by their fathers, mothers, and other ancestors, in like manner and form as any other child or children born in lawful matrimony shall or may inherit, or be inheritable according to the course of inheritances used in this realm; and be it further enacted, that the said John Manners, called Lord Roos, shall be entitled to be a tenant by courtesy of the lands and inheritance of such wife whom he shall hereafter marry; and such wife as he shall so marry shall be entitled to dower of the lands and tenements whereof the said John Manners, called Lord Roos, shall be seised of such estate whereof she shall be dowable as any other husband or wife may or might clayme, have, or enjoy; and the child or children born in such marriage shall and may derive and make title by descent or otherwise to and from any of their ancestors, as any other child or children may do, any law, statute, restraint, prohibition, ordinance, canon, constitution, prescription, or customs had, made, exercised, or used to the contrary of the premises, or any of them, in anywise notwithstanding.

Did the Bill pass, even though only by a narrow majority, because of the laxer moral atmosphere after the Restoration or had Milton's views had some influence? He was consulted as an expert on divorce during the passage of the Bill by two of its supporters. Did Charles II watch the debate merely for amusement? Burnet writes:

In the reformation of the ecclesiastical laws, that was proposed by Cranmer and others, in King Edward's time, a rule was laid down, allowing of a second marriage upon divorce for adultery. This matter had lain asleep above a hundred years, till the present Duke of Rutland, then Lord Roos, moved for the like liberty. At that time a sceptical and libertine spirit prevailed; so that some began to treat marriage only as a civil contract, on which the Parliament was at full liberty to make what laws they pleased; and most of King Charles's Courtiers approved of this, hoping, by this doctrine, that the King might be divorced from the Queen. The greater part of the bishops apprehending the consequences that Lord Roos's Act might have, opposed every step that was made in it; though many of them were persuaded that, in the case of adultery, when it was fully proved, a second marriage might be allowed.

It is said that Charles II supported the passing of the Bill. It seems much more doubtful whether he hoped that it might set a precedent for himself. Lady Roos had committed adultery. The Queen was barren. If the Queen had committed adultery it would have been treason and a capital crime. In any event it looks as though the passing of the first Private Bill for Divorce may well have been due at least in part to the combined efforts of a puritan poet and a profligate king. Although it will probably never be known for certain why Lord Roos was enabled to get his historic precedent it was one which other powerful men were soon to follow. In 1700 there was passed an 'Act to Dissolve the marriage of Henry, Duke of Norfolk, Earl Marshal of England, with the Lady Mary Mordaunt, and to enable the said Duke to marry again'.

In 1820, another king not noted for his sexual continence attempted to follow the precedents set by his subjects. George IV wished to be rid of his Queen Caroline, the purity of whose life was also in doubt. Henry Brougham, who supported the Queen's cause, offered to do his best to keep the Queen out of the country if he were made a K.C. His offer was not accepted by the Government. According to E. L. Woodward:

> The cabinet introduced a bill to dissolve the king's marriage, and thereby to deprive the queen of her title; a public inquiry into the queen's conduct thus became a necessary stage in passing the bill. The inquiry lasted from 17 August until the early part of November, and the bill was passed in the house of lords by a small majority. It was clear that the peers thought the queen guilty, but doubted the expediency of the divorce. The cabinet decided that there was little chance of getting their bill through the commons, and dropped it.

Gradually as the number of Private Bills increased during the eighteenth century it came to be established that before promoting a Private Bill the husband must normally first have brought successfully an action for damages in the Common Law Courts against the man with whom his wife was alleged to have committed adultery and then obtained a decree of separation in the Ecclesiastical Courts.

The action for damages was called an action for criminal conversation and the wife had no right to be heard in the proceedings. By collusion between the husband and an obliging nominal Co-respondent a wife could therefore be framed, or an obliging wife could collude with her husband. Writing of these actions the Royal Commission Report of 1853 said:

> In the majority of actions which are brought against adulterers, judgment is allowed to go by default. This admits the defendant's guilt; and it only remains for the plaintiff shortly to prove the facts before the sheriff and a common jury, when damages are assessed as of course. In these cases it usually happens that no counsel appears for the defendant. The facts, therefore, sworn to, are admitted without inquiry; the witnesses are subject to no cross-examination; the cause is heard ex parte. What security against fraud is afforded by such a proceeding? If the parties are anxious to collude, what is to prevent the plaintiff from receiving the damages with his right hand, and then, as soon as the Bill of Divorce has passed, returning them with his left? It is obvious that an action so conducted, and a verdict so obtained, are utterly undeserving of reliance or attention, in considering the merits of a Divorce Bill.

In any event in 1776 there had been heard in Westminster Hall the case of the Duchess of Kingston who, in the words of Lord Birkenhead: 'wanted, as people of means and position always do, a shorter way which would give her all the advantages of a divorce with none of the exposure or delay'.

It was the most famous trial of the century. The Duchess was tried by her Peers and pressure for seats to see the spectacle was enormous. She was tried and found guilty of bigamy. The history of the various matrimonial proceedings which led to this climax reeked of collusion.

Late at night on 4 August 1744 the Duchess, then Miss Chudleigh, had secretly married Augustus John Hervey, a younger son of the Earl of Bristol. In 1759 when it looked as though her husband might succeed to the earldom of Bristol steps were taken to procure and preserve evidence of her secret marriage. The Earl, however, then recovered his health and by 1768 when Augustus John had succeeded to the earldom, his wife had a chance of becoming a duchess having been the mistress of the Duke of Kingston for some time past. Both husband and wife now wanted to rid themselves of the secret marriage. The Earl proposed to obtain a decree *a mensa et thoro* in the Ecclesiastical Courts on the grounds of his wife's adultery and then follow this up with a Private Act of Parliament. He was anxious to take the proceedings with his wife's co-operation. The following is an extract from the evidence of Ann Craddock at the trial in 1776:

> 'Had you any conversation with the prisoner, about the year 1768, about any message to be delivered to the prisoner that Mr. Hervey had given to you . . . ?'
> 'I told her Mr. Hervey desired me to let her know that he was determined to be, I should have said divorced, but I said parted; and also that he desired me to tell the lady she had it in her own power to assist him. I delivered the message, and the lady replied "Was she to make herself a whore to oblige him?"'

Through another messenger the Earl informed her:

> that her lawyers, either with or without herself, might, in conjunction with his lawyers, look over all the depositions, and that if any parts were found tending to indecent or scandalous reflections, which his gentleman of the law should think might be omitted without weakening his cause, he himself should have no objection to it; that as he intended only to act upon the principles of a gentleman and a man of honour, he should hope she would not produce any unnecessary or vexatious delays to the suit or enhance the expenses of it, as he did not intend to prosecute to gain by any demands of damages . . .

Whereupon his wife brought a suit in the Ecclesiastical Courts and by suppressing material evidence obtained a judgment to the effect that she had never been married to the Earl. She then married the Duke and her troubles only began after the Duke's death when someone who was disappointed with the Duke's will started making inquiries into her past life.

That Parliament was well aware of the possibility of a false case having been concocted by a husband is shown by the fact that in two cases in 1801 and 1807 where the husbands had each received substantial damages their Private Bills were rejected. Conversely, in one case in 1811, when the husband had failed in his claim for damages his Bill was passed. Speaking in the House of Lords on 20 May 1856 Lord Brougham said that he could cite a case:

in which in an action for crim. con. the defendant's family compounded with the plaintiff by paying him £50, and a verdict was taken in the absence of the wife, by which she was condemned unheard. Further proceedings, however, took place in the Ecclesiastical Court, where it was shown, not only that the adultery had not happened, but that it was impossible it could have happened, as there never had been consummation either by the husband or any other man. In the meanwhile the poor woman had lain under the imputation for eighteen months. This might be an extreme case, but it was not an extreme case to suppose that the peace and reputation of women might be destroyed in those actions where they were neither heard nor represented.

By 1798 the House of Lords had drawn up the most elaborate Code of Procedure to govern the presentation of Private Bills. The wife had every opportunity of being heard if she wished to oppose the Petition. No Petition for leave to bring in a Private Bill could be presented unless an official copy of the proceedings and sentence of the Ecclesiastical Court had been delivered at the bar of the House of Lords. A report of any civil proceedings had to be transmitted by the judge. The Petitioner had to attend on the Second Reading to be examined at the bar as to whether there had been collusion relative to the adultery, or between him and his wife or any other party in connection with the Bill, the proceedings in the Ecclesiastical Court or the proceedings for criminal conversation. The practical effect of these rules is shown by a case in 1801 when the case was dealt with on the following separate occasions:

9 Feb. 1801	Leave given for petition to lie upon the Table
2 Mar.	Order made for substituted service
5 Mar.	Petition to be taken into consideration and the Lords summoned
13 Mar.	Copies of Ecclesiastical Court proceedings brought to House of Lords
	Leave given to bring in a Bill
	Bill read first time
30 Mar.	Bill read a second time. Witnesses called and examined by Counsel
14 Apr.	Further consideration of Bill adjourned
17 Apr.	Further evidence by witnesses
21 Apr.	Adjourned
24 Apr.	Legal argument

27 Apr.	Adjourned
8 May	Adjourned
11 May	Adjourned
13 May	Adjourned
18 May	Bill committed to Committee of the whole House
20 May	House in Committee
22 May	House in Committee
27 May	Bill with amendments ordered to be engrossed
28 May	Bill passed in House of Lords

The Bill was then subjected to a similar procedure in the House of Commons where it was amended and sent back to the House of Lords on 13 June 1801. On 23 June the House of Lords accepted the amendments made by the House of Commons and on 23 June the Bill received the Royal Assent. In this particular case from the time when the Petition was first presented to the House of Lords until it received the Royal Assent took only four and a half months which is less than some undefended Petitions take today and the day after the Bill received the Royal Assent the Petitioner was free to remarry. However, the preliminary proceedings in the Ecclesiastical Courts and the action for criminal conversation might and often did take years. And the cost of this elaborate rigmarole was enormous. As to this the Royal Commission of 1850 reported:

> Three tribunals must now be resorted to: a Court of Law for damages against the adulterer; an Ecclesiastical Court for a Divorce ā mensā et thoro; and the Imperial Parliament for a dissolving statute. The great expense and the long delay of these proceedings is a grievous hardship and oppression to individuals, and they amount in many cases to a denial of justice. Even in an unopposed suit, the minimum expense of obtaining a sentence of Divorce in the Consistory Court of London would vary from £120 to £140 at the least, and the case would occupy about two months. If it were opposed, the expense would range from £300 to £500 and upwards (in heavy cases to much more), and it would take from one to two or three years before it was decided. The proceedings also do not terminate here; but there is an appeal to the Court of Arches, and from thence to the Judicial Committee. The expense of an action-at-law will depend in a great measure on the nature of the case, and the extent to which it is contested. The expenses in Parliament, exclusive of counsel's

fees, charges for witnesses, and the solicitor's own bill, which amount, no doubt, to a considerable sum, average about £200. With the other charges they would possibly be doubled; so that the total cost, under the most favourable circumstances, of obtaining a Divorce ā vinculo matrimonii can hardly be less than £700 or £800; and when the matter is much litigated, it would probably reach some thousands. In Scotland the average cost of rescinding a marriage is said to be £30, and that when there is no opposition, £20 will suffice. In Scotland, also, it is not a privilege for the rich, but a right for all; and it is not unworthy of notice that out of ninety-four cases between November, 1836, and November, 1841, the parties litigant were almost all of the lower classes.

If one translates the above figures into present-day values it will be realized that even when everything went as smoothly as possible the cost was enormous.

The form of a husband's Petition for a Private Bill is shown by the following copy of an actual Petition dated 1 March 1821:

To The Right Honourable the Lords Spiritual and Temporal of the United Kingdom of Great Britain and Ireland in Parliament assembled—

The humble Petition of William Miller of Ozleworth otherwise called Ouzleworth in the County of Gloucester Esquire:

Sheweth

That your said Subject on the ninth Day of July One thousand eight hundred and nine intermarried with Frances Wyndham Spinster one of the Daughters of The Honourable William Frederick Wyndham that they lived together as Man and Wife from that time till the Month of March now last past.

That in the said Month of March your said Subject discovered that the said Frances his Wife had entered into a Criminal intercourse and adulterous conversation with Richard Hawker of Dudbridge in the County of Gloucester aforesaid Esquire and since that time your said Subject hath not cohabited or had any intercourse with the said Frances his wife.

That your said Petitioner did in Easter Term last bring his action in His Majestys Court of Kings Bench at Westminster against the said Richard Hawker for such criminal intercourse and adulterous conversation with the said Frances and hath obtained Judgment in the said Action for the Sum of One thousand and Two hundred Pounds which hath been fully paid to your said Subject.

That your said Petitioner in the Month of June last exhibited a Libel in the Consistory Court of Gloucester against the said Frances Miller and on the first Day of February now last past obtained a Definitive Sentence of Divorce from Bed Board and mutual cohabitation against the said Frances Miller in the said Court, for the adultery by her committed.

That the said Frances Miller hath by her adulterous behaviour dissolved the Bond of Marriage on her part and your Petitioner is deprived of the Comforts of Matrimony and remains liable to have a spurious Issue imposed upon him to succeed to his Estates and Fortune unless the said Marriage is declared void and annulled by Parliament.

Your Petitioner therefore most humbly prays that leave may be given to bring in a Bill to dissolve the Marriage of your said Petitioner with the said Frances Miller and to enable him to marry again.

William Miller
March 1st 1821.

In subsequent chapters I set out the form of the Petition at later stages in the history of divorce. It will be seen that although the contents slowly change, the form of the Petition remains remarkably resilient. Whether this is yet one more example of the lawyer's alleged inbuilt conservatism or of the English love for tradition I do not know. In the Petition set out above you will have noticed that the Petitioner specifically refers to having brought successfully an action for criminal conversation and to having obtained a decree in the Ecclesiastical Courts. What I should like you to ponder on for a moment or two is the last paragraph before the prayer for relief in which the Petitioner says that he is 'liable to have a spurious Issue imposed upon him'. These words are very important. With only a very few exceptions the Private Bill procedure was not only limited to persons of enormous wealth. It was also limited to husbands and then only to the ground of adultery. It was so limited because the common view was that expressed by Dr. Johnson in the following passage from Boswell's *Life of Johnson*:

I mentioned to him a dispute between a friend of mine and his lady, concerning conjugal infidelity, which my friend had maintained was by no means so bad in the husband as in the wife.

Johnson: 'Your friend was in the right, Sir. Between a man and his Maker it is a different question: but between a man and his wife, a husband's infidelity is nothing. They are connected by children, by fortune, by serious considerations of community. Wise married women don't trouble themselves about infidelity in their husbands.'

Boswell: 'To be sure there is a great difference between the offence of infidelity in a man and that of his wife.'

Johnson: 'The difference is boundless. The man imposes no bastards upon his wife.'

This attitude and the practice of normally allowing only the husband to petition solely for adultery affected the legal position of wives until 1923.

In 1801 Mrs. Addison became the first wife to succeed in getting a divorce enabling her to remarry by Private Act of Parliament. Her husband had committed adultery with her married sister. That sister's husband brought an action for criminal conversation successfully against Mr. Addison. Mrs. Addison succeeded in persuading Parliament to let her Bill pass because her husband had committed not merely adultery but incestuous adultery. In supporting her case Lord Thurlow used the law of affinity in her favour. By marrying Mrs. Addison, and subsequently having sexual intercourse with her sister Mr. Addison created a situation whereby if he thereafter had sexual intercourse with his own wife he would be committing incest with her.

In 1831 Mrs. Turton also succeeded in getting a Private Bill through where her husband had committed adultery with her sister. In a case in 1842 the husband had, to his knowledge, at the time of the marriage an 'infamous disease' which he communicated to his wife. Within three weeks of the marriage he had committed adultery which he repeated frequently and openly. He then committed bigamy and was sentenced to be transported to New South Wales. His wife's Private Bill succeeded. Mrs. Moffatt in the following year was not so fortunate. Despite the fact that Mr. Moffatt committed adultery on the night of the marriage, seduced female domestics, cohabited with a prostitute, lived with her in Belgium, assumed her name and was a drunkard, Mrs. Moffatt's Bill was voted against by sixteen to nine. Lord Brougham, though generally on the side of reform, thought that for a wife to succeed, something far worse than Mr. Moffatt's conduct was needed—otherwise he foresaw that any man who wanted to get rid of his wife would merely have to take a mistress.

The pattern therefore became established—a husband could petition on the ground of adultery and for him all would go through smoothly. A wife had to establish more than adultery and could only expect to be allowed to petition successfully in the most exceptional circumstances such as when the adultery was incestuous.

As we have seen, the wife had no right to take part in the preliminary action by her husband for criminal conversation. In the Ecclesiastical Courts the evidence was not given orally but 'upon written answers to written interrogatories, where the second and every succeeding question is propounded to the witness without the propounder knowing what answer has been given to the first'. Commenting on this practice F. A. Inderwick wrote in 1862:

> The Ecclesiastical Courts . . . examined the witnesses in secret, away from the judge who tried the cause, and who, having their depositions alone before him, could only guess at their credit and their impartiality, on the principle of certain doctors of the seraglio, who profess to discover the ailments of their patients by mere inspection of their palms.

At least under the Private Bill procedure the allegedly guilty wife had an opportunity of giving oral evidence in her own defence in the House of Lords.

When the Ecclesiastical Court granted a separation decree they also determined the amount of maintenance the wife was to have. During the proceedings the husband was ordered to pay alimony—usually at the rate of about one-fifth of his income. The allowance at that stage was less because during the proceedings the wife was expected to live 'in a state of retirement or seclusion'. When it came to deciding on permanent alimony the innocent wife was awarded sometimes a half and sometimes one-third or less of the husband's income. If the parties did not agree the wife had to file a document setting out her husband's means. In the Courts today a similar function is performed by an Affidavit of Means which also gives details of the party's own financial position. I set out below an example of an Allegation of Faculties taken from the *Practice of the Ecclesiastical Courts* by H. C. Coote published by Butterworth in 1847.

In the Consistory of London.

On the fourth session of Michaelmas Term, to wit, Friday the 6th day of December, 1844.

LEGGE against LEGGE

On which day Orme, in the name, and as the lawful proctor of the said Sarah Legge, the lawful wife of Henry Legge, and under that denomination, and by all better and more effectual ways and means, and to all intents and purposes in the law which may be most beneficial to his said party, said, alleged, and in law articulately propounded, as follows, to wit.

First.   That the said Henry Legge has for many years, and now continues to carry on, at Nos. 143 and 144, Old Street, in the parish of Saint Luke, in the county of Middlesex, the trade or business of a manufacturer of and dealer in cigars. That he employs, or lately employed, in the said trade, one shopman, one porter, and twenty apprentices, and also a man to overlook the said apprentices; and that he also employs two commission travellers. That the net annual income and profits arising from such business, after deducting all expenses of carrying on same and other outgoings, amount on an average to the sum of £1,000 or £800 per annum, or thereabouts, or at least £600, or some other large sum of lawful money of Great Britain; and this was and is true, public, and notorious; and so much the said Henry Legge doth know in his conscience to be true; and the party proponent doth allege and propound of any other annual income as shall appear from the lawful proofs to be made in this cause, and every thing in this and the subsequent articles of this allegation contained, jointly and severally.

Second.   That the said Henry Legge now is or lately was possessed of cash in the hands of bankers, or other persons in trust for him, and also in his own possession, amounting in the whole to the sum of £1,000, or some other large sum of lawful money of Great Britain; and this was and is true, public, and notorious; and the party proponent doth allege and propound as before.

Third.   That divers persons are in debt to the said Henry Legge in several sums of money, amounting in the whole to the sum of £3,000, or at least £2,500, or some other large sum of lawful money of Great Britain; and this, etc.

Fourth. That the said Henry Legge now is or lately was possessed of a valuable stock in trade for carrying on his aforesaid business of a cigar manufacturer, amounting in value to the sum of £2,000, or some other large sum of lawful money of Great Britain; and this, etc.

Fifth. That the said Henry Legge now is or lately was possessed of household furniture, plate, linen, china-ware, horses, and other effects, altogether of the value of £200, or thereabouts, of lawful money of Great Britain; and this, etc.

Sixth. That the said Henry Legge is possessed of, or entitled to, several capital sums of money standing in his own name, or in the name or names of some other person or persons, in trust for him, in some or one or more of the public stocks, funds, or securities, or the stock of the Bank of England, or of the East India Company, or some other security, to the amount altogether of the sum of £1,000, or some other sum, of lawful money of Great Britain; and this, etc.

Seventh. That all and singular the premises were and are true, public, and notorious; and so forth.

The financial position of the wife under the Private Bill procedure is summarized in the Report of the Royal Commission in 1853 as follows:

Parliament may mould and adapt its relief according to the facts and exigencies of the case. In former times, it was asked to provide, by express enactment, that the divorced wife should not be left in a state of destitution. According to the modern practice, this is a matter that is ordinarily effected by private arrangement; but it is never neglected. 'There is in the House of Commons . . . a functionary called "The Ladies' Friend" . . . whose duty it is to see that the husband petitioning for Divorce makes some suitable but moderate provision for the divorced wife.' This he attends to on all occasions; not by inserting the intended provision in the Bill itself . . . but by taking care that it is legally secured to her, before the Bill has passed through Committee.

Commenting on this in 1858 John MacQueen wrote:

The parliamentary practice of requiring the injured husband to make a provision for his delinquent wife had not much to recommend it either morally or legally. Morally, it seems monstrous to compel a man to support through life the woman who has dishonoured him; legally she has no claim whatever because after she has committed adultery, her husband may turn her out of doors. . . .

The usage commenced at an early period, when the complainants were generally men of figure and station, whose wives, though culpable, had in the legislative body relatives and friends who stood out for terms—divorce being a bounty unknown to the law. . . . In this way what was no doubt startling at first, came in time to be regarded as not wholly unreasonable, especially where the wife was of high rank, where she had brought a fortune to her husband and where withal her dereliction was accompanied by palliating circumstances.

One final peculiarity about the Private Bill procedure is noteworthy. Under a standing order of the House of Lords, despite the rejection of its Bill to this effect in 1771, it was provided that no Bill to disallow a marriage on the ground of adultery should be received unless it contained a clause prohibiting the marriage of the guilty parties. But having been inserted, this clause was almost invariably struck out before the Bill was enacted. *The Times* called it 'legislative hocus pocus'.

Looking at the position from the point of view of the wife it can be summarized by saying that for practical purposes she had no right to divorce whatsoever, however frequently her husband committed adultery, whereas he could divorce her as of right for one act of adultery. If she were divorced some small financial provision might be made for her. One other thing might have been expected to concern her—then as now—the children. Again the position can be summarized shortly. She had no rights whatsoever to custody or access.

In her *Letter to the Queen* in 1855 Caroline Norton, Sheridan's granddaughter, explained what a mother's position was:

. . . at length I left my husband's for my sister's house. He wrote then, adjuring me to pardon him . . . he vowed to treat me kindly for the future. To my lasting injury I 'condoned'. My family, however, did not choose to resume terms of intimacy with him and he quarrelled with me on that account. I insisted on my right to take my children to my brother's house, though my brother would not receive him. Those children were kidnapped while I was with my sister and sent by my husband to a woman who has since left him money, and of whom he knew I had the worst opinion . . . that vile woman, who threatened to give me 'to the police' when I went there and claimed them.

It was not till six weeks after the stealing of my children—and after having attempted to condition that if my family would retract all that had been said against him, he would retract all he had said against me—that Mr. Norton took higher ground than his real cause of anger—and appeared before the world in the character of 'an injured husband'. . . . He brought an action against Lord Melbourne—who was in no way connected with our quarrel: who had been a most kind friend to us and with whom, the last time I had ever seen him in my home—my husband was on the best possible terms, endeavouring to procure from him a loan of money! . . . Lord Melbourne declared that, so far as Mr. Norton was concerned, he believed the action to be brought entirely as a means of obtaining money. And, as to the persons who were known to have instigated the proceedings, he considered it was a political plot on the part of a small section of the Tories—to ruin him as Prime Minister.

At the trial, it was proved that the witnesses for the 'injured husband' had received money, and had actually resided till the time of trial at the country-seat of Lord Grantley, Mr. Norton's elder brother. The jury listened with incredulity and disgust at the evidence; and without requiring to hear a single witness for Lord Melbourne, or leaving the jury-box, they instantly gave their verdict against Mr. Norton; a verdict which was received with cheers which the judge could not suppress; so vehement was the expression of public contempt and indignation. . . .

After the trial was over Mr. Norton notified me that my family might support me, or that I might write for my bread; and that my children were by law at his sole disposal.

We have had a look at divorce by the Private Bill procedure and we can see embodied in it rules of law, practice and procedure and fossilized social attitudes which were to affect the development of the law over the next hundred years. In England change occurs not by revolution but by piecemeal Act and amending Act always and inevitably late to respond to a changing social climate. The new Act will be a compromise between what the more ardent reformers seek and what can be steered through Parliament in the face of opposition. Large chunks of the pre-existing law are preserved wholly intact or only slightly changed.

Even the procedure by Private Bill continued to survive until 1939 as the sole means of obtaining a divorce for Northern Ireland citizens.

3

DIVORCE FOR THE MIDDLE CLASS— THE FORSYTE SAGA ERA

What [our marriage law] is really founded on is the morality of the tenth Commandment, which Englishwomen will one day succeed in obliterating from the walls of our churches by refusing to enter any building where they are publicly classed with a man's house, his ox, and his ass as his purchased chattels. In this morality female adultery is malversation by the woman and theft by the man, whilst male adultery with an unmarried woman is not an offence at all.
GEORGE BERNARD SHAW: From the Preface to *Getting Married* (1908)

> *I will be master of what is mine own;*
> *She is my goods, my chattels, she is my house,*
> *My household stuff, my field, my barn,*
> *My horse, my ox, my ass, my anything.*
> WILLIAM SHAKESPEARE: *The Taming of the Shrew*

Would men but generously snap our chains, and be content with rational fellowship instead of slavish obedience, they would find us more observant daughters, more affectionate sisters, more faithful wives, more reasonable mothers—in a word, better citizens. We should then love them with true affection, because we should learn to respect ourselves. . . .

I lament that women are systematically degraded by receiving the trivial attentions which men think it manly to pay to the sex, when, in fact, they are insultingly supporting their own superiority.
MARY WOLLSTONECRAFT: *A Vindication of the Rights of Woman* (1792)

[Women] are so far in a position different from all other subject classes, that their masters require something more from them than actual service. Men do not want solely the obedience of women, they want their sentiments. All men, except the most brutish, desire to have, in the woman most nearly connected with them, not a forced slave but a willing one, not a slave merely, but a favourite. . . . The law of servitude in marriage . . . is the sole case now that negro slavery has been abolished,

in which a human being in the plenitude of every faculty is delivered up to the tender mercies of another human being. . . . Marriage is the only actual bondage known to our law. There remain no legal slaves, except the mistress of every house. . . .

If the family in its best forms is, as it is often said to be, a school of sympathy, tenderness, and loving forgetfulness of self, it is still oftener, as respects its chief, a school of wilfulness, overbearingness, unbounded selfish indulgence, and a double-dyed and idealised selfishness, of which sacrifice itself is only a particular form: the care for the wife and children being only care for them as parts of the man's own interests and belongings, and their individual happiness being immolated in every shape to his smallest preferences.

JOHN STUART MILL: *On the Subjection of Women* (1869)

In a criminal case heard on Assize in about 1844 Mr. Justice Maule said:

Prisoner, you have been convicted of the grave crime of bigamy. The evidence is clear that your wife left you and your children to live in adultery with another man, and that you then intermarried with another woman, your wife being still alive. You say that this prosecution is an instrument of extortion on the part of the adulterer. Be it so; yet you had no right to take the law into your own hands. I will tell you what you ought to have done; and, if you say you did not know, I must tell you that the law conclusively presumes that you did. You ought to have instructed your attorney to bring an action against the seducer of your wife for criminal conversation. That would have cost you about a hundred pounds. When you had recovered (though not necessarily actually obtained) substantial damages against him, you should have instructed your proctor to sue in the Ecclesiastical Courts for a divorce a mensa et thoro. That would have cost you two hundred or three hundred pounds more. When you had obtained a divorce a mensa et thoro, you should have appeared by counsel before the House of Lords in order to obtain a private Act of Parliament for a divorce a vinculo matrimonii which would have rendered you free and legally competent to marry the person whom you have taken on yourself to marry with no such sanction. The Bill might possibly have been opposed in all its stages in both Houses of Parliament, and altogether you would have had to spend about a thousand or twelve hundred pounds. You will probably tell me that you never had a thousand farthings of your own in the world; but, prisoner, that makes no difference. Sitting here as an English judge, it is my duty to tell you that this is not a country in which there is one law for the rich, and another for the poor. You will be imprisoned for one day, which period has already been exceeded as you have been in custody since the commencement of the Assizes.

The above often quoted and celebrated passage is a pungent summary of the existing state of the law by a humane judge and was quoted in the subsequent debates in Parliament on a new Divorce Bill. In 1850 a Royal Commission was appointed

to inquire into the present state of the law of Divorce in this country, and more particularly into the mode of obtaining Divorce a vinculo matrimonii in this country

(i.e. a divorce enabling the parties to remarry). The Chairman was Lord Campbell who stated in the House of Lords that the object was not to alter the law but the procedure by which the law was carried into effect. The Commissioners recommended that in future it should be possible for a man to obtain in a Court of Law a decree of divorce on the ground of his wife's adultery but they were opposed to giving a wife a right to divorce solely on the ground of her husband's adultery. The Bill gave effect to these recommendations.

Proceedings in Parliament were protracted. The out and out opponents of the Bill were against it on religious grounds and because they feared that the first Bill would lead to others. Some of the supporters of the Bill tried to achieve equality for women. In the House of Lords Lord Lyndhurst said:

It is said that if equal facilities of divorce were given to women the Courts would very soon be choked up with their applications. But I know woman's character better than that. I know that in none but extreme cases would she resort to this remedy. . . . But, in principle, there ought to be no distinction made between the adultery of the husband and that of the wife.

In the Commons, Gladstone, who personally believed in the indissolubility of marriage and who strongly opposed the Bill, said that he wanted the law of the Church to be left alone and for there to be a separate civil form of divorce and remarriage. He argued that there were many causes for divorce 'far more fatal' than adultery to the great obligations of marriage such as disease, idiocy and crime involving imprisonment for life and he was in favour of equality of the sexes.

In a leading article on 15 August 1857, *The Times*, which was in favour of the Bill, was not pleased with Mr. Gladstone:

> The social questions involved in the Divorce Bill are of great importance, and the incidental results of the voluminous debates on the subject are in themselves not insignificant; but the country, while it is deeply interested in the dignity of the House of Commons, cannot regard with absolute indifference the suicidal vagaries of its most eloquent member. The wanton sacrifice of a great reputation is a public loss, as well as a melancholy spectacle. Great ability is not common, but practical wisdom is a still rarer and more precious quality. Mr. Gladstone has of late done his utmost to prove that mental subtlety, far from indicating the presence of good sense and of temper, may become a positively mischievous faculty.
>
> On Thursday last the House was engaged for ten hours in discussions on a single clause in the Divorce Bill, and in that time, including questions, explanations, and interlocutory suggestions, Mr. Gladstone made nine and twenty speeches, some of them of considerable length. Sometimes he was argumentative, frequently ingenious and critical, often personal, and not less often indignant at the alleged personality of others. Finally, he closed the debate with a vehement attack upon Lord Palmerston, on the ground of certain supposed taunts, which of course were declared to be incapable of disturbing his temper. It is probable that some of his arguments may have been well founded, and possible that it may have been judicious to urge them; but no purpose, except that of defeating the Bill by waste of time, could account for twenty-nine distinct appeals to the attention of the Committee.

And on another occasion *The Times* commented:

> Mr. Gladstone's extraordinary power of oratory was again displayed by his success in riveting the attention of the House of Commons during a long theological disquisition which was at the same time minute and irrelevant.

If Gladstone could have foreseen how divorce was to affect his own political career some thirty years later he might have fought the Bill even harder, if that were possible.

Eventually, under the premiership of Palmerston, the Bill passed as the Matrimonial Causes Act 1857, the Attorney-General refusing to accept any major amendments in the House of Commons. He said:

> We are now, however, limited to the performance of that duty which this Bill imposes on us—namely, to erect a new tribunal and to embody the principles of law which already exist . . . this present Bill need not be the end-all of legislation upon the subject. By this Bill we shall create a tribunal which may hereafter have to administer other laws made under happier auspices.

Writing in July 1857 Lord Campbell said:

> I am very glad that the Divorce Bill finally passed the Commons framed almost exactly according to the recommendations of the Commission over which I had the honour to preside—preserving the law as it has practically subsisted for two hundred years; that a husband who has conducted himself properly may obtain a dissolution of the marriage for the adultery of the wife, and that a wife may obtain a dissolution of the marriage for the adultery of the husband attended by incest or any aggravation which renders it impossible for the connubial union to continue; the law being now to be administered by a regular judicial tribunal, instead of the injured parties being obliged to petition the legislature for Private Acts of Parliament to dissolve the marriage. We were assailed on the one hand by those who hold that according to the divine law marriage cannot be dissolved even for adultery, and on the other by those who think that for this purpose no distinction should be made between the sexes, and that in all cases the wife should be entitled to a divorce on proof of any breach of the marriage vow by the husband. But I think the true principle is, that the marriage ought only to be dissolved when it is impossible for the injured party to *condone*, and that Divine Providence has constituted an essential difference in this respect between the adultery of the husband and the adultery of the wife. I would rather run the risk of cases of great hardship occurring when it would seem desirable that women should be released from the tyranny of profligate and brutal husbands, than give too great a facility to divorce, which has a tendency most demoralising.

Eighteen months later he was writing in different terms:

> . . . I have been sitting two days in the Divorce Court and, like Frankenstein, I am afraid of the monster I have called into

existence. . . . Upon an average, I believe there were not in England above three divorces a year a vinculo matrimonii, and I had no idea that the number would be materially increased if the dissolution were judicially decreed by a Court of Justice instead of being enacted by the Legislature. But I understand that there are now 300 cases of divorce pending before the new court. This is rather appalling. In the first place, the business of the court cannot be transacted without the appointment of fresh judges; and there seems some reason to dread that the prophecies of those who opposed the change may be fulfilled by a lamentable multiplication of divorces, and by the corruption of public morals.

History was to show that both those who opposed the Bill because it would be the first step down a slippery slope and those of its supporters who thought it was unsatisfactory were right. Although the Bill was presented to Parliament as if it only represented a change in procedure and although this was true, the 1857 Act was the great watershed.

It was a bad time for the Church. In 1855 the jurisdiction of the Ecclesiastical Courts in defamation had been removed and in 1857 it lost its jurisdiction in testamentary matters and in cases of intestacy which was transferred to a newly created Court of Probate. Now the jurisdiction in matrimonial causes was also taken away with the result that all cases, whether only for separation or for divorce, had to be heard in London. On the voyage of the *Beagle*, Darwin had already laid a sea mine which was to explode in his *Origin of Species* in 1859.

But although jurisdiction was taken away from the Ecclesiastical Courts the law and practice of those Courts was taken over by the newly-created Court. Section 6 of the Matrimonial Causes Act 1857 provided:

As soon as this Act shall come into operation all jurisdiction now vested in or exerciseable by any Ecclesiastical Court or person in England in respect of divorces a mensa et thoro, suits of nullity of marriage, suits for restitution of conjugal rights, or jactitation of marriage, and in all causes, suits and matters matrimonial, except in respect of marriage licences, shall belong to and be vested in Her Majesty, and such jurisdiction, together with the jurisdiction conferred by this Act, shall be exercised in the name of Her Majesty in a Court of Record to be called 'The Court for Divorce and Matrimonial Causes'.

During the debates in Parliament before the Bill was passed great stress was laid on the importance of having a new tribunal of the highest possible stature. Accordingly, section 8 provided that the judges were to be the Lord Chancellor, the Lord Chief Justice of the Court of Queen's Bench, the Lord Chief Justice of the Court of Common Pleas, the Lord Chief Baron of the Court of Exchequer, the senior puisne Judge for the time being in each of the last three Courts mentioned and the Judge of the Court of Probate.

Section 27 gave the new Court power to grant decrees of divorce enabling the parties to remarry. But section 22 said:

> In all suits and proceedings, other than proceedings to dissolve any marriage, the said Court shall proceed and act and give relief on principles and rules which in the opinion of the said Court shall be as nearly as may be conformable to the principles and rules on which the Ecclesiastical Courts have heretofore acted and given relief. . . .

The result was that the law on such matters as adultery, cruelty and desertion was still largely governed by principles worked out in the Ecclesiastical Courts. Even now the judges frequently have to consider what the law was long before 1857.

In a case in 1967 (*Padolecchia* v. *Padolecchia*, [1968] P. 314), for example, the Court had to consider the nature of the jurisdiction of the Ecclesiastical Courts. The judge pointed out that their jurisdiction was 'exercised *pro salute animae*—for the sake of the souls of the parties who were before the Courts' and that the jurisdiction depended on the presence of the party with the salvation of whose soul the Court was concerned within the territorial area over which the Court exercised its power. The judge then considered the Ecclesiastical jurisdiction Act of 1531 and went on to deal with the post-Reformation distinction drawn by the Ecclesiastical Courts between void and voidable marriages and explained that the Common Law Courts had not always seen eye to eye with the Ecclesiastical Courts on the technicalities concerning the law of impediments to marriage. Finally in this part of his judgment he specifically referred to section 22 of the 1857 Act of which he said:

> There is high authority to establish first, that the effect of section 22 was to vest in the new court the cumulative jurisdic-

tions of the ecclesiastical courts which it had superseded . . . and, secondly, that although section 22 was repealed by the . . . Supreme Court of Judicature (Consolidation) Act, 1925, section 32 of the Act of 1925 has a similar effect to section 22 of the Act of 1857.

Like Maitland's forms of action, so far as matrimonial cases are concerned, the Ecclesiastical Courts have been buried but still rule us from their graves.

With the passing of the 1857 Act the opportunity for divorce on very restricted grounds was now theoretically open to all. Lord Campbell may have been appalled by the rush of applicants although by present-day standards we may think that the rate of increase was modest. Even as late as 1901–5 the average annual number of Petitions for dissolution and for nullity was only 812. Were the vast majority of Victorian marriages ideally happy, or was it that the introduction of divorce in a Court of Law coincided with one of those periodic swings in English public opinion from permissive to puritan? Or was it that for most people divorce was still too expensive?

Whether or not the present much higher rate of divorce reflects in any way a decline in religion or morals since Victoria's reign seems incapable of proof one way or another or even of reasoned argument. From a study of English history I gain the general impression that in some periods public opinion has been more or less hostile to sexual freedom. I feel, rightly or wrongly, that there was a different atmosphere after the Restoration from that prevailing under Cromwell and that in the Regency period things were not quite the same as in the later Victorian period. On the other hand it may be that the public tone of a decade does not necessarily accurately reflect the behaviour of most private individuals during the same period. I suspect that adultery and fornication did not vanish under Cromwell and I do not suppose that most married men could afford to beget as many bastards as Charles II. While the Prince Regent was building his stately pleasure dome at Brighton, the Wesleyan revival was working through the country. While Victoria was parading the virtues of family life, Palmerston was looking in the wrong bedroom at Windsor Castle for his mistress.

Writing of the Evangelicals, G. M. Young says:

> By about 1830 their work was done. They had driven the grosser kinds of cruelty, extravagance, and profligacy underground. They had established a certain level of behaviour for all who wished to stand well with their fellows. In moralizing society they had made social disapproval a force which the boldest sinner might fear.

However, their influence does not seem to have reached the costermongers of London of whom Mayhew in his *London Labour and the London Poor* which was first published in 1851 wrote:

> Only one-tenth—at the outside one-tenth—of the couples living together and carrying on the costermongering trade are married. . . . Of the rights of 'legitimate' or 'illegitimate' children the costermongers understand nothing, and account it a mere waste of money and time to go through the ceremony of wedlock when a pair can live together, and be quite as well regarded by their fellows, without it. The married women associate with the unmarried mothers of families without the slightest scruple. There is no honour attached to the marriage state, and no shame to concubinage. Neither are the unmarried women less faithful to their 'partners' than the married; but I understand that, of the two classes, the unmarried betray the most jealousy.
>
> As regards the fidelity of these women I was assured that, 'in anything like good times', they were rigidly faithful to their husbands or paramours; but that, in the worst pinch of poverty, a departure from this fidelity—if it provided a few meals or a fire—was not considered at all heinous. . . . The fidelity characterizing the women does not belong to the men.

Unlike the Evangelicals but like Eliza Doolittle's father they would have replied to the question 'Have you no morals?'— 'Can't afford them, Governor.'

Perhaps the main reason, apart from expense, why the rate of divorce did not increase more rapidly before the First World War, was connected with the general legal position of women, her restricted property rights and her inability to achieve financial and sexual independence.

Meanwhile, three other events had taken place which were to affect the position of women as much as, if not far more than, the first stage in the modern history of divorce. Mary Wollstonecraft's *Vindication of the Rights of Woman*, published in 1792, had advocated education for girls—'Women', she said, 'might certainly study the art of healing, and be physicians as well as nurses.' In 1828 a series of lectures for women was given at University College, London. In 1849 Mrs. Jessica Reed took a house in Bedford Square which was the first beginnings of Bedford College. In 1850 the North London Collegiate was founded under Miss Buss. During the Crimean War itself—and not the least remarkable feature of the Matrimonial Causes Act 1857 is that it was being debated in Parliament during and immediately after the Crimean War and during the Indian Mutiny—Florence Nightingale had taken the first major step in the long road to establish the right of upper and middle class women to make something better of their lives than sitting at home doing needlework or painting third-rate water colours.

And in 1854 a book by Dr. George Drysdale was published originally entitled *Physical, Sexual, and Natural Religion*. Dr. Drysdale affirmed that sexual abstinence was 'infinitely more unnatural' than 'preventive sexual intercourse' and that impregnation and childbirth were 'of the very greatest importance to the health and happiness of woman . . . hence every woman should produce her fair share of offspring; but it is probable that two or three children during life would be quite sufficient to secure these advantages'. He asked:

> Is man ready to renounce all sexual intercourse except that of marriage? Then let him ask of woman to do the same; but if he be resolved to have a freer and more dignified state of sexual relations than at present exists he can only do so by giving the woman exactly an equal share of freedom.

He was of the opinion that even at the time he wrote methods of birth control were 'very common' and he went on to discuss specific methods such as the rhythm system, coitus interruptus, sheaths, the introduction of some substance such as a piece of sponge into the vagina and post-coital douches. He said that: 'any preventive means, to be satisfactory, must be used by the woman, as it spoils the passion and impulsiveness of the veneral act, if the man has to think of them'.

He would have been delighted by the Pill and welcomed recent trends—

It is absolutely impossible to have a free, sincere, and dignified sexual morality in our society, as long as marriage continues to be the only honourable provision for the union of the sexes, and as long as the marriage bond is so indissoluble as at present.

The book sold eighty thousand copies by the end of the century and reached its thirty-fifth edition in 1905. The results were striking. By 1869 Lecky was writing:

The belief that a rapid increase of population is always eminently beneficial, which was long accepted as an axiom by both statesmen and moralists . . . has now been replaced by the directly opposite doctrine, that the very highest interest of society is not to stimulate but to restrain multiplication, diminishing the number of marriages and of children.

By 1877 the birth rate began to fall. Of this, R. C. K. Ensor writes:

Most authorities are now agreed that by far the largest (though not the sole) cause of the fall in the English birth rate since 1877 was that people learned to use contraceptives.

and he has analysed the available statistics to show that the fall in the birth rate was greater in the upper and middle classes than in other classes. He wrote:

The more successful and prosperous classes fell rapidly behind in their contribution to the future personnel of the nation. Such a strong and growing tendency to non-survival amongst the fittest stocks is not known to have before occurred in England, at any rate since the Reformation.

What then was the position about divorce between 1857 and the next major step in 1923? The most important thing to realize is that a wife still did not have the same rights to divorce her husband as the husband had to divorce his wife. The only ground available to either was adultery—the husband had to prove adultery by his wife and nothing more. Except in the cases of rape, sodomy or bestiality, the wife had to prove not only her husband's adultery, but in addition one of the following: bigamy, desertion for at least two years, cruelty or incest.

The theoretical disparity between the positions of the wife and husband was modified to some extent in practice since, according to evidence given to the Royal Commission of 1909–12, once a wife had established that her husband had committed adultery, a jury might be willing to find that he had also been cruel on fairly slender evidence. However, the difference between the legal rights of the wife and husband was consistent with the spirit of the age which regarded adultery by a wife as something far worse than adultery by a husband. It was also consistent with the previous practice which had grown up under the procedure for divorce by Private Act of Parliament.

In distinguishing between the consequences of adultery by a husband and a wife the Victorian legislators of 1857 were concerned to protect the family from an infiltration by bastards. If the husband commits adultery with another woman that woman may be single, married, divorced or a widow, but if he gets her with child the unfortunate illegitimate child remains outside his family home. If the wife is got with child by a man other than her husband she introduces illegitimacy into his family home. She also introduces uncertainty. There have been several recent cases before the Courts where neither the wife, husband or Co-respondent has been certain who is the father of the child and the Courts have had to determine whether blood tests should be ordered to determine the paternity of the child. Such progress has been made with blood testing in recent years that it is now often but not always possible to determine with certainty who is the father as well as who is not the father. Sometimes the adulterous wife deliberately introduces uncertainty. There has been more than one case where a wife who has displayed a marked reluctance to have sexual intercourse with her husband for a long time, has suddenly invited him to have sexual intercourse on one or two occasions. Eight or nine months later a child has been born and the wife has gone to live with the other man. The husband has petitioned for divorce and the wife has remarried. She has then claimed custody of the child on the ground that the Co-respondent is the father. On the other hand, if she had been left in the lurch by her lover, the child could, and probably would, have been passed off as the child of her husband.

The distinction between the effect of adultery by a husband and by a wife is similar to the distinction between polygamy and polyandry which was helpfully illustrated for me by the Moslem gentleman who tried to teach me Urdu at Bangalore in 1944. Sometimes as we sat on the veranda outside the mess we would, as a rest from our labours, discuss such topics as the Moslem doctrine of marriage which permits the husband to have four wives but not a wife to have four husbands. What, I would say, could be unfairer than that? He did not answer the question directly but smiled gently and said: 'Suppose you have one teapot and four tea cups and you pour the tea from the pot into the cups. Now suppose you have one tea cup and four tea pots and you fill the tea cup from the four tea pots. In the first case you know where all the tea has come from. . . .' He did not need to finish the sentence.

Perhaps the Victorians, although apparently unfair to women, had a point.

The Matrimonial Causes Act 1857 came into effect on 1 January 1858. Many unhappy spouses had been consulting their lawyers before then and among the quickest off the mark was a Birmingham manufacturer named George Wells. On 5 March 1858 his Petition was filed. It was number One hundred and twenty-four. It contained a sad story of six children, two of whom 'died in early infancy' and of a mother who drank and committed adultery. Here it is:

In the Court for Divorce and Matrimonial Causes
To the Court for Divorce and Matrimonial Causes
and
To the Judge Ordinary and other Judges of Her Majesty's Court
for Divorce and Matrimonial Causes
The second day of March One thousand
eight hundred and fifty eight.
The humble Petition of George Wells now residing at Acocks Green in the Parish of Yardley in the County of Worcester and carrying on business at Buckingham Street Birmingham in the County of Warwick Steel Pen Manufacturer

SHEWETH

1st   That your Petitioner was on the twenty fifth day of August one thousand eight hundred and thirty six married to Eliza

Wells, then Eliza Hubball spinster, at the Parish Church of Yardley aforesaid.

2nd   That after his said marriage your Petitioner lived and cohabited with his said wife at Birmingham aforesaid and that your Petitioner and his said wife had issue of their said marriage six children altogether, namely two sons and four daughters, two of whom, that is to say: Agnes and Rosa died in early infancy, and the remainder are now living, namely: Alfred Frederick aged twenty one years in December last, Ellen aged seventeen years in August last, Agnes aged fifteen years in November last and William George aged fourteen years in February last.

3rd   That during the cohabitation of your Petitioner and his said wife she unhappily became addicted to habits of intoxication and your Petitioners family and children were in consequence thereof much neglected—such habits became the subject of much complaint and unhappiness on the part of your Petitioner. In the month of November one thousand eight hundred and forty seven your Petitioner and his said wife were residing and cohabiting at Lozells Lane Birmingham aforesaid. Your Petitioner was ill for some time and confined to his bed and when he recovered he found that various articles of his property had been pawned or disposed of by his said wife without his knowledge or consent and the proceeds thereof spent in drink and that your Petitioner's said wife had also contracted many debts for liquors at Public houses in the neighbourhood.

4th   Your Petitioner upon making this discovery went to the house of his Brother in Law and partner in trade John Hinks of Birmingham aforesaid Steel Pen Maker to ask his advice taking with him his Daughter Agnes now living then aged about five years. The said John Hinks came back with him to his house and remonstrated with your Petitioner's said wife and informed her that he considered your Petitioner was bound to make arrangements for the proper care and protection of his children—That your Petitioner thereupon took with him another Child, namely, William George now living and then aged about three years and placed him together with his said Daughter Agnes under the care of Sarah the wife of Edward Brattan of Birmingham aforesaid your Petitioner's Sister

5th   Your Petitioner on returning home on the evening of the same day found that his said wife had left his house taking with her her own wearing apparel and also his said eldest daughter

Ellen then aged about six years and also Rosa his youngest Child then an infant at the breast and who died about three months afterwards. Your Petitioner about two days afterwards found the said Child Ellen deserted in the Street in the Town of Birmingham. Your Petitioner took possession of her and has since maintained and provided for her and all your Petitioner's said other living children.

6th   Your Petitioner has never since his said wife left your Petitioner's house as before mentioned cohabited with her or had any carnal intercourse with her or had any personal communication with her or seen her except on one or two occasions casually in the Street when she may have accosted him but your Petitioner has on all such occasions refused to hold and did not hold any personal communication with her.

7th   Your Petitioner's said wife after she so left your Petitioner in November one thousand eight hundred and forty seven committed adultery with a person or persons to your Petitioner unknown at Birmingham aforesaid and on or about the twenty eighth day of March one thousand eight hundred and fifty one was delivered of a male child. The birth of the said Child was registered by her on the seventh day of May one thousand eight hundred and fifty one pursuant to the Act in that behalf with the Registrar of the District of All Saints Birmingham under the name of Frederick Hubball the name of the Father being stated as George Hubball and the Mother as Eliza Hubball formerly Harrison. The said child was kept and supported by your Petitioner's said wife until the month of October one thousand eight hundred and fifty four when the said Child died and was buried by your Petitioner's said wife at the Old Cemetery in Birmingham aforesaid. The said death of the said Child was registered with the Registrar of the District of Saint George's Birmingham on the twenty sixth day of October one thousand eight hundred and fifty four by one Joshua Whiting with whom as hereinafter mentioned your Petitioner's said wife was then cohabiting, the said child being therein described as Frederick Hubball Son of Eliza Hubball Dress maker and the said burial is entered in the Register book at the said Cemetery under the date October twenty ninth one thousand eight hundred and fifty four as of Frederick Hubball aged three years the Child of Eliza Hubball. That such Child was not the child of your Petitioner as your Petitioner had not had any carnal intercourse with his said wife for three years and upwards before the birth thereof.

8th   That some time in the year one thousand eight hundred and
fifty three your Petitioner's said wife formed an adulterous
intercourse with one Joshua Whiting of Birmingham aforesaid
Carpenter and cohabited with the said Joshua Whiting as his
wife in lodgings in the house of one   Kirby situate near
the Saltley Works near Birmingham aforesaid. She thenceforth
continued to cohabit with the said Joshua Whiting in lodgings
in the house of the said   Kirby in Hospital Street Birmingham aforesaid and afterwards in a house situate in Heath Street
near the Smethwick Works Birmingham aforesaid. That during
the last twelve months she has been cohabiting with the said
Joshua Whiting as his wife at a house situate in Garbett Street
in Birmingham aforesaid. About the twenty second day of
January One thousand eight hundred and fifty five your
Petitioner's said wife was delivered of a Female child which is
still living and is called Lizzy Whiting. That she caused the
birth of the said child to be registered with the Registrar of the
District of All Saints Birmingham aforesaid on the first day of
March one thousand eight hundred and fifty five under the
name as respects the said Child of Eliza Rosina Whiting and
that in the entry in the Register Book of the said Registry the
name of the Father is stated as Joshua Whiting and the name of
the Mother as Eliza Whiting late Wells formerly Hubball.
That such Child was not the child of your Petitioner as your
Petitioner had not had any carnal intercourse with his said
wife for seven years and upwards prior to its birth

Your Petitioner therefore humbly prays that your Lordships
will be pleased to decree that your Petitioner's said marriage
with his said wife be dissolved
And that your Petitioner may have such further and other
relief in the premises as to your Lordships may seem meet.
And your Petitioner will ever pray etc.

Signed by the said George Wells ⎫
   the Petitioner in the presence ⎪
   of me ⎪
   ⎪
      Edwin Wright ⎬   GEORGE WELLS
      of Birmingham ⎪
   ⎪
Attorney and Solicitor for the ⎪
said George Wells in the matter ⎪
of this Petition. ⎭

So far as the wife's position after 1857 was concerned it was slightly improved by the Matrimonial Causes Act 1884. As we have seen in the Ecclesiastical Courts a deserted spouse could obtain a decree of restitution of conjugal rights which ordered the deserter to return and to render conjugal rights. After 1813 a sentence of imprisonment not exceeding six months was substituted for the previous sentence of excommunication. The Act of 1884 abolished punishment by imprisonment for failure to comply with a restitution decree. . . . 'Instead,' in the words of the Law Commission, 'such failure to comply was deemed to be desertion (known as 'statutory desertion'), entitling either spouse to an immediate decree of judicial separation and, if coupled with the husband's adultery, entitling the wife to an immediate divorce.'

Bearing in mind the combined effect of the Acts of 1857 and 1884 we are now in a position to appreciate the problem which faced Soames Forsyte when his sister Winifred Dartie told him of her husband Monty's departure to South America with 'the Spanish filly'.

What did Soames do? He first checked to make sure that Monty had really gone. Then he decided to have him shadowed to get evidence of adultery. He then asked Winifred whether there had been any cruelty, since to succeed in an action for divorce she needed to prove adultery and some other ground, one of which was cruelty. He questioned Winifred about cruelty but she was reluctant to involve the children. Then he briefly touched on legal separation but rejected it because 'you're both married and unmarried'. Finally he came to the Act of 1884—

> 'It must be divorce,' he said decisively, failing cruelty, there's desertion. There's a way of shortening the two years, now. We get the Court to give us restitution of conjugal rights. Then if he doesn't obey, we can bring a suit for divorce in six months' time. Of course you don't want him back. But they won't know that. Still, there's the risk that he might come. I'd rather try cruelty.'
>
> Winifred shook her head. 'It's so beastly.'
>
> 'Well,' Soames murmured, 'perhaps there isn't much risk so long as he's infatuated and got money. Don't say anything to anybody, and don't pay any of his debts.'

And so it was decided that Winifred would go ahead with a Petition for restitution of conjugal rights. To start the ball rolling he wrote out a letter for Winifred to copy to her husband.

Dear Montague,
 I have received your letter with the news that you have left me for ever and are on your way to Buenos Aires. It has naturally been a great shock. I am taking this earliest opportunity of writing to tell you that I am prepared to let bygones be bygones if you will return to me at once. I beg you to do so. I am very much upset, and will not say any more now. I am sending this letter registered to the address you left at your club. Please cable to me.

Your still affectionate wife,
Winifred Dartie.

Pausing there for a moment, I may perhaps be allowed to comment that having seen similar letters drafted for clients to send to their spouses this effort of Soames's does not strike me as particularly convincing. Even making allowances for the more stilted language of the Victorian era, it strikes me as suspiciously like a formal, dictated letter and not the heartfelt cry of a woman for her man. But however convincing an effort may be produced by a professional adviser, or even by the spouse, and however genuine its contents, its effect is apt to be considerably reduced when a wide awake judge asks the Petitioner when he or she first consulted solicitors and compares that date with the date on the letter. To establish desertion, unsolicitored testimonials are best. But to return to Soames and Winifred. Her Petition for Restitution of Conjugal Rights would have been filed and might have looked like this:

In the High Court of Justice
Probate Divorce and Admiralty Division
 (Divorce)
The 26th day of August 18——

To The Right Honorable The President of the said Division

 The Petition of Winifred Dartie of Green Street in the City of Westminster the lawful wife of Moses Montague Dartie

SHEWETH

1   That your Petitioner was on or about the 31st day of May 1879 lawfully married to the said Moses Montague Dartie at the Parish Church of St. George's, Hanover Square, in the County of Middlesex.

2   That after her said marriage your Petitioner lived and co-habited with the said Moses Montague Dartie at divers places and at Green Street aforesaid and that there is issue of the said marriage now living namely Val Dartie born the 2nd day of June 1880, Imogen Dartie born the 3rd day of September 1882, Maud Dartie born the 15th day of December 1884 and Benedict Dartie born the 18th day of May 1886.

3   That the said Moses Montague Dartie hath ever since the 14th day of March 1892 withdrawn from cohabitation with your Petitioner and has kept and continued away from her without any just cause whatever and has refused and still refuses to render her conjugal rights.

> Your Petitioner therefore humbly prays that your Lordship will be pleased to decree that your Petitioner was on the 31st day of May 1879 lawfully married as aforesaid to the said Moses Montague Dartie and that the said Moses Montague Dartie do return to her and render to her conjugal rights.

> And that your Petitioner may have such further and other relief in the premises as to your Lordship may seem meet.
> Winifred Dartie.

The Petition came on and Winifred got her decree but not without one or two tricky moments when the judge started probing. Val, Winifred's son,

> followed with a certain glee the questions framed so as to give the impression that she really wanted his father back. It seemed to him that they were 'foxing Old Bagwigs finely'. And he had a most unpleasant jar when the Judge said suddenly:
> 'Now, why did your husband leave you—not because you called him "the limit", you know?'

For a minute or two things were in the balance. How well I know how Soames felt—you are sailing along quite smoothly when suddenly the placid stream turns a corner and all at once your client and you are nearly shipwrecked in a totally un-expected judicial cataract. Viewers of the B.B.C. television serialization of *The Forsyte Saga* may remember how marvellously this courtroom scene was acted, the look in the judge's eyes, the momentary anxiety passing across Winifred's face. However, all was well. She got her decree. Unfortunately before she could go on to the next stage and get a divorce decree Monty turned up again and what did Soames say then?

'Hoist with our own petard. Why the deuce didn't you let me try cruelty? I always knew it was too much risk this way.'

To say 'I told you so' at such a time does not seem the most shining example of brotherly affection.

You may have noticed that whilst under the Private Act procedure the applicant had to go round the mulberry bush three times, Winifred Dartie had to go round twice. Even now many people for various reasons do the same. They obtain an order in the Magistrates' Court or a decree of judicial separation and then later in separate proceedings go for divorce.

But supposing Winifred Dartie had gone on to get a divorce decree as others in her position did—what happened about the children and what was the position about property rights?

Whatever differing views people may hold about the indissolubility of marriage or divorce on various grounds such as divorce by consent or after five years' separation, everyone agrees that the break-up of the family is a tragedy for the children. Debate continues on whether it is better for children to live under the same roof as their parents whose marriage has broken down or whether it is better for the parents to split up and the children to be shared in time between them. Most parents are still attached to their children even though their marriage has failed. Some parents are perhaps even more attached to their children because the marriage has failed, desperately anxious to preserve at least some of the family ties of love, hoping to compensate by even greater devotion to the children for the sense of failure in the relationship between parents and sometimes, as a consequence, entering into a parental competition for the children's affections which one suspects the children are quick to sense and take advantage of as some small compensation for the wrecking of their home. What many parents fail to realize is that if both parents are attached to the children there will be a continuing and sometimes very difficult relationship between the parents which may go on for ten or fifteen years after the divorce. The parents look to the divorce to end a situation of intolerable strain between them—sometimes the intolerable strain carries over and affects the children and the parents even after the divorce when for years many of the factors which led to dispute when the parents were together may lead to fights over access, clothing, schooling, doctors and dentists.

I do not think that parents often deliberately and consciously use the children to continue their war after the divorce although it sometimes looks like this. I think that the views which they have formed of each other during the marriage and particularly during the period of breakdown which precedes the divorce inevitably colour their views of each other after divorce. The strains and suspicions feed on themselves and sometimes are fed by the children.

Sometimes a parent decides to walk out of his or even her children's lives altogether because it is thought to be less strain on the children for them to be with one parent only. Sometimes as they grow older the children will seek out the parent who has disappeared and establish a happy relationship.

Fortunately it is only in a minority of cases that bitter fights over the children develop. But in nearly all cases where there are children, whichever parent consults a solicitor wants to know very early on what his or her position will be with regard to the children after a divorce and whether it will make a difference as to who successfully petitions or cross-petitions. It is at this stage that the solicitor begins to talk about custody, care and control, staying and visiting access and such questions as parental choice of schooling, and the sharing of school holidays. For years I have found difficulty in explaining the difference between custody, and care and control to clients and in explaining precisely what custody means. It was some consolation therefore to find that in the recent case of *Hewer* v. *Bryant*, [1969] 3 W.L.R. 425, even Lord Denning, Master of the Rolls, and two other Lord Justices of Appeal, both of whom are also very experienced in divorce work seemed to find the precise meaning of 'custody' a little difficult to define. Lord Denning expressed the wish 'that Parliament had told us what it meant by the words "in the custody of a parent". They have aroused acute controversy.' Lord Justice Sachs said:

In their efforts to assist the court counsel referred to the series of words and phrases appearing in that cascade of legislation which during the past half century has touched upon the welfare and protection of children from many angles. In those statutes one finds scattered, sometimes with and sometimes without definitions, words and phrases such as 'care, control, custody, actual custody, legal custody, guardian, legal guardian and possession'. *In the end, so far as comprehensibility on these matters is concerned, one finds that this voluminous and well intentioned legislation has created a bureaucrat's paradise and a citizen's nightmare.* . . .

Before proceeding further, *it is essential to note that among the various meanings of the word 'custody' there are two in common use in relation to infants which are relevant that need to be carefully distinguished. One is wide—the word being used in practice as almost the equivalent of guardianship; the other is limited and refers to the power physically to control the infant's movements.*

In its limited meaning it has that connotation of an ability to restrict the liberty of the person concerned. . . . This power of physical control over an infant by a father in his own right qua guardian by nature and the similar power of a guardian of an infant's person by testamentary disposition was and is recognized at common law; but that strict power (which may be termed his 'personal power') in practice ceases upon his reaching the years of discretion. When that age is reached, habeas corpus will not normally issue against the wishes of the infant. . . .

This strict personal power of a parent or guardian physically to control infants, which is one part of the rights conferred by custody in its wider meaning, is something different from that power over an infant's liberty up to the age of 21 which has come to be exercised by the courts on behalf of the Crown as parens patriae. . . .

Similarly that personal power of a parent needs to be distinguished from those which may be conferred on him by courts exercising their jurisdiction under the Matrimonial Causes Acts.

In its wider meaning the word 'custody' is used as if it were almost the equivalent of 'guardianship' in the fullest sense—whether the guardianship is by nature, by nurture, by testamentary disposition, or by order of a court. (I use the words 'fullest sense' because guardianship may be limited to give control only over the person or only over the administration of the assets of an infant.) Adapting the convenient phraseology of counsel, such guardianship embraces a 'bundle of rights', or to be more exact, a 'bundle of powers', which continue until a male infant attains 21 [now 18], or a female infant marries. These include power to control education, the choice of religion, and the administration of the infant's property. They include entitlement to veto the issue of a passport and to withhold consent to marriage. They include, also, both the personal power physically to control the infant until the years of discretion and the right (originally only if some property was concerned) to apply to the courts to exercise the powers of the Crown as parens patriae. *It is thus clear that somewhat confusingly one of the powers conferred by custody in its wide meaning is custody in its limited meaning, namely, such personal power of physical control as a parent or guardian may have*. . . .

The trouble is that while the legislature has distinguished between guardianship and custody, the courts have tended often to use the latter word as if it were substantially the equivalent of the former, thus leading to some confusion of thought. This confusion is abetted by the language of the Matrimonial Causes Acts and orders made under them. *Whatever may have been the intention of the legislature when first using that word when in section 35 of the Matrimonial Causes Act 1857, it referred to 'custody, maintenance, and education', the courts have come to give more than one meaning to it in orders.* An unqualified order giving custody to a parent appears nowadays to be interpreted as having the wide meaning, but if at the same time 'care and control' is given to the other parent, then one of the powers, custody in the limited meaning of physical control, is taken out of 'custody' in the wide meaning. *It would be a happier situation if by future legislation the courts were enabled to use the word 'guardianship' in orders in appropriate cases.*

Lord Justice Karminski said:

The words which have to be considered in this case are 'in the custody of a parent'. The meaning of these words is indeed obscure. *Custody by itself may have a wide variety of meanings, but we are here concerned only with parental custody. I agree with Sachs L. J. that some of the difficulties of the present case stem from the tendency of courts in the past to equate guardianship with custody. Further difficulties arise from the modern practice of ordering, in appropriate cases, custody to one parent and care and control to the other parent. This form of order indicates that in some way custody and care and control are quite separate things. I do not think that they are*. . . .

From the passages which I have italicized in the above extracts from the judgments the only thing which emerges with crystal clarity is that the whole situation now is as clear as mud. Was it any clearer in Winifred Dartie's time?

At the beginning of the nineteenth century the right of the father to the custody of his legitimate infant child was almost unrestricted. In a case in 1804 the father had forcibly taken an eight-months-old child, still at breast, from the mother. The father was allowed to keep the child. The fact that the mother had separated from the father was regarded in itself as a factor against her. Even if the mother had obtained a decree in the Ecclesiastical Courts against the father on the grounds of adultery he could still get custody of the children unless he brought them into contact with the woman. Not only did the father get custody—that is physical custody of the children—if he wanted it, even when he had been guilty of matrimonial misconduct and even in the case of a child of eight months, he could also get support from the Courts in preventing his wife having access unless he had previously agreed to let her have it. But even if he agreed in a Deed to give custody of the children to his wife the Court treated such a clause as not binding on him.

To some slight extent the situation was different where proceedings were brought in the Court of Chancery as distinct from proceedings on a writ of habeas corpus in a Court of Common Law. Avowedly the Court of Chancery proceeded on the principle that in dealing with infants the main consideration should be what was for their benefit but the Court started with the assumption that it was for their benefit to be in the custody of their father—in the words of Lord Justice Bowen as late as 1883 (*Re Agar Ellis* (1883), 24 Ch.D. 317):

> It is not the benefit to the infant as conceived by the Court, but it must be the benefit to the infant having regard to the natural law which points out that the father knows far better as a rule what is good for his children than a Court of justice can.

In another case in 1847 (*Re Spence* (1847), 2 Ph. 247) the Lord Chancellor, Lord Cottenham, said:

> It does not follow that because a husband's conduct is such as to make his wife very unhappy that he is therefore to be deprived of the custody of his children. To justify such interference with the father's rights, his misconduct must appear to be of such a nature as to be likely to contaminate and corrupt the morals of his children.

55

Once again the change was gradual, being brought about partly by statute and partly by a change in the climate of public opinion which in turn was reflected through the different attitudes taken by judges of different generations.

An Act of 1839 empowered the Lord Chancellor and the Master of the Rolls to hear applications for access by mothers when the father had custody provided there had been no finding of adultery against the wife in an action for criminal conversation or in an ecclesiastical suit. The Matrimonial Causes Act 1857 gave the Court power in matrimonial proceedings to make such orders 'as it may deem just and proper with respect to the custody, maintenance, and education of the children the marriage of whose parents is the subject of [the] suit or other proceedings'.

In 1873 the Custody of Infants Act gave the Chancery Court power to make orders in respect of custody and control and access in favour of a mother when the infant was not over sixteen years of age. Adultery by the mother was no longer to be a bar. Section 5 of the Guardianship of Infants Act 1886 enacted that the Court—which included the County Court—in making orders for custody and access, should have regard to the welfare of the infant, and to the conduct of the parents and to the wishes as well of the mother as the father.

It will be noticed that even now the Court was not directed to make the welfare of the infant the primary consideration.

So far as the Divorce Court was concerned the prevailing attitude was summed up in a case in 1862 (*Seddon* v. *Seddon and Doyle* (1862), 2 SWJ Tr. 640). A husband petitioned for divorce on the ground of his wife's adultery and claimed £3,000 damages against the Co-respondent. The jury found the wife guilty of adultery but also found that the husband had been guilty of adultery, wilful neglect and misconduct conducing to his wife's adultery. They showed what they thought of him by assessing damages at a farthing. The judge said:

> The Petitioner has come before the Court in a most unfavourable character. His conduct towards the unfortunate respondent was most heartless. Jealous by nature, that unhappy woman had her jealousy constantly kept alive by her husband, and at last threw herself into the arms of her seducer. She must take the consequences of her conduct. It will probably have a

salutary effect on the interests of public morality, that it should be known that a woman, if found guilty of adultery, will forfeit, as far as this Court is concerned, all right to the custody of, or access to her children. . . .

Commenting on this case in Rayden the Editors write:

'This rule, which now seems little less than outrageous, and was never deemed applicable to a man, was applied with unmitigated severity for nearly fifty years.' Even after 1910 'the Court displayed great reluctance to order access to a guilty wife, where the husband objected'.

What were married women's property rights during the nineteenth century? 'The laws respecting woman', wrote Mary Wollstonecraft, 'make an absurd unit of a man and his wife; and then, by the easy transition of only considering him as responsible she is reduced to a mere cypher.' It would be a fair summary of a highly technical department of law then still based on feudal law to say that except in the case of the few women owning land or whose families consulted lawyers, what belonged to the husband was his and what belonged to the wife was also his, and his absolutely to dispose of as he thought fit. In a sense there was Community of Property since all property went into one pot—but the pot and its contents belonged to the husband.

What did this mean in real life? When there was a happy marriage and a husband prudent in financial matters perhaps no harm was done. And it does not follow that because the legal ownership was the husband's the actual control was necessarily always his—there were no doubt then, as now, strong-willed wives who neither knew nor cared what the law might say and who ran their homes, their husbands and the family business. The Wife of Bath has explained how she used Lysistrata's methods to secure her financial advantage.

But tel me this, why hidestou with sorwe
The keys of thy cheste away fro me?
It is my good as wel as thyn, pardee
What, weenestou make an idiot of oure dame?
Now by that lord that called is Saint Jame,
Thou shalt nought bothe, though that thou were wood,
Be maister of my body and of my good:
That oon thou shalt forgo, maugree thine yën

But not everyone was as tough or resourceful a character as the Wife of Bath. Speaking in the debates on the Matrimonial Causes Bill 1857 Lord Lyndhurst said that where a wife was judicially separated—

> if the wife tries to eke out a scanty subsistence for herself and her children by the exercise of any art in which she is proficient, or by instruction, the husband can seize upon the proceeds of her industry and bestow them upon his mistress.

This remained the position for some years after 1857 for that majority of wives who were not judicially separated from their husbands. He could control her freehold land, dispose of her leaseholds during his lifetime and any personal belongings or money she had or earned belonged to him absolutely.

Caroline Norton pointed out in 1855 that the wife's property was the husband's, that he could claim her earnings and that she might not leave her husband's house—

> Not only can he sue her for restitution of conjugal rights but he has a right to enter the house of any friend or relation, with whom she may take refuge, and who may 'harbour' her—as it is termed—and carry her away by force. . . .
>
> The marriage ceremony is a civil bond for him—and an indissoluble sacrament for her. The rights of mutual property which that ceremony is ignorantly supposed to confer, are made absolute for him, and null for her.

However, just as a few of the wealthy had been able to get a divorce by Private Act of Parliament before 1857 so the landed classes took steps to protect their family interests and those of their womenfolk by obtaining treatment for them which was exceptional to the general law. As early as the sixteenth century the Court of Chancery had introduced a rule which enabled property to be transferred to a married woman 'for her sole and separate use' free from the control of her husband. Of this Mr. Justice Megarry writes:

> The invention by Equity of 'the separate use' made it possible for a married woman to deal by herself with property subject to such a use, but it did not protect her from yielding to the asperities or blandishments of her husband and conveying the property to him, nor did it protect her against her creditors if she were improvident. Consequently, Equity made it possible on the grant

of property to a married woman for the grantor not only to give it for her separate use but also to subject it to a restraint on anticipation. . . . An effective restraint on anticipation prevented the married woman from disposing of or charging the capital or future income in anyway. Each instalment of income could be disposed of as soon as it was paid, but neither the married woman nor her creditors could attack the capital or future income.

Slowly—as in the case of divorce itself—what had been the prerogative of the wealthy with regard to married women's property rights was extended by Act of Parliament to all classes.

The 1857 Act itself protected for the future the property which wives acquired during a judicial separation or after a protection order on the ground of desertion. In the same year Lord Brougham sought to protect the position of married women generally. Speaking in the House of Lords on 13 February 1857 he said:

> It may be in the recollection of your Lordships that I last Session presented a petition, with which I had the honour to be intrusted, from two thousand and upwards of our fellow countrywomen of all classes; some supporting themselves by the wages of their daily labour; some having property bestowed upon them by the kindness of friends, or the testamentary bounty of persons deceased; others earning gains to a considerable, even to a large amount by their industry and their talents . . . and all such gains are only in name theirs of whose toil and whose skill they are the produce. All in reality belong by our law's decrees to the husband, all are vested in him by right, and he may at his own good pleasure vest them also in possession; nay never having in the least degree helped their production, he may without the delay, the respite of an instant, or one word of notice or warning, or even demand, seize upon the whole, sweep all away, and leave her who created the whole stript of them to the very last farthing. He may squander them upon his pleasures, lavish them on his paramour, employ them to support his spurious progeny, and there exists not the possibility of his being in any the very least degree either controlled or even called to account for the heartless cruelty of his robbery, or his profligate use of its fruits.
>
> Such is the law of England, and of this law we complain. But I have the greater confidence in my prospect of obtaining the concurrence of this House in our views, because your Lordships and your connections are not those on whom its pressure weighs so heavily. In your fortunate position, with the protection which

settlements and the interposition of trustees afford, the grievance is felt, but it is comparatively slight; above all the worst part of the evil can hardly be felt in any way, for that refers to the earnings of labour and of skill, for the exertion of which for their support your wives are happily relieved. It is not upon the families of those whom I now address, or of persons generally in the upper ranks of society, but upon the middle classes and the humbler order of our fellow citizens that the evil falls, to crush their most deserving members, while it protects and even encourages the worst in their idleness or their profligacy.

Lord Brougham's effort failed but others, including John Stuart Mill, took up the campaign for reform. Mill's book *On the Subjection of Women* was published in 1869 and in 1870 the Married Women's Property Act gave the wife the right to keep all her own earnings, and some very restricted rights to keep for herself property derived through a deed, a will or an intestacy. In 1882 the Married Women's Property Act of that year made the great breakthrough. From then on all property of a married woman was to be her separate property solely under her legal ownership and control although until 1925 a conveyance or bequest of property to a husband and wife and a third person resulted in the husband and wife getting one half jointly and the third person the other half.

Restraints on anticipation continued to be possible until the end of 1935 and were not finally abolished until 1949 under the Labour Government after a Private Bill dealing with the particular case of Lady Mountbatten had been initiated and abandoned. The reason for the abolition of restraints on anticipation was to enable wealthy women to take steps to reduce liability to estate duty. It being felt that the procedure to establish a private right by Private Bill was something of an anachronism by 1949, a general Act was passed. However, the fact remains that nearly one hundred years after the 1857 Act had abolished the Private Bill procedure for obtaining a divorce, the Private Bill procedure was used in an attempt to obtain an exception to the general law in favour of a wealthy person.

By 1882, statute, following the path already trodden by Equity in the Court of Chancery, had established the right of a married woman to possess separate property over which her husband had no control. A vital and significant victory had been won in the fight to establish equal rights for women. The Victorian progressives might well have felt satisfied with their reforming efforts. In fact what they had done was to ensure that in future there would be no community of goods or property between wife and husband; each would retain his or her own separate property—if any. Commenting in 1964 the President of the Probate Divorce and Admiralty Division, Sir Jocelyn Simon, said:

... Men can only earn their incomes and accumulate capital by virtue of the division of labour between themselves and their wives. The wife spends her youth and early middle age in bearing and rearing children and in tending the home; the husband is thus freed for his economic activities. Unless the wife plays her part the husband cannot play his. The cock bird can feather his nest precisely because he is not required to spend most of his time sitting on it.

In such a state of affairs a system of Separation of Goods between married people is singularly ill adapted to do justice. Community of Goods or at least Community in acquisitions and accumulations, is far more appropriate. And as one leaves the sphere of those who enjoy investment property for that of those whose property largely consists of the home and its contents a régime of Separation is utterly remote from social needs.

The first attempt to bring the principle of Community of Property into English law was not made until 1968 when Mr. Edward Bishop introduced his Matrimonial Property Bill into the House of Commons. Although it passed through the House of Commons the Bill was rejected in the House of Lords on the grounds that the consequences of introducing the principle of Community had not been sufficiently carefully thought out, that the Bill was badly drafted and that the whole question of matrimonial property was being looked at by the Law Commission. It is certainly true that where Community of Property has been established there are often great practical difficulties in taking accounts as between husband and wife when the marriage breaks down, and that countries which have Community of Property usually allow the spouse to contract out of Community. Mr. Bishop's Bill contained a similar provision.

But we must now return to look at what was happening in the law of divorce towards the close of the Forsyte Saga era.

4

DIVORCE BEFORE A. P. HERBERT

If we take a document like Pepys' Diary, we learn that a woman may have an incorrigibly unfaithful husband, and yet be much better off than if she had an ill-tempered, peevish, maliciously sarcastic one, or was chained for life to a criminal, a drunkard, a lunatic, an idle vagrant, or a person whose religious faith was contrary to her own. . . . Adultery, far from being the first and only ground for divorce, might more reasonably be made the last, or wholly excluded.
GEORGE BERNARD SHAW: From the Preface to *Getting Married*
(1908)

Apart from the difference between the rights of the two sexes which was established in the Divorce Act, the Act is a manifestly imperfect one. If divorce is admitted at all, on utilitarian grounds, there are reasons quite as strong as adultery for granting it. It is a scandal to English legislation that it should not be granted where one of the partners has been condemned for some grave criminal offence involving a long period of imprisonment or penal servitude, or for wilful and prolonged desertion, or for cruelty, however atrocious, if it is not coupled with adultery.
W. E. H. LECKY: *Democracy and Liberty* (1896)

Although the rate of divorce did not increase after 1857 as much as it might have done if the moral and social climate had been different the increase alarmed many people. Matrimonial proceedings received wide publicity from newspapers which were not then, as they have been since 1926, prevented from reporting the evidence given at the trial. As early as 26 December 1859 Queen Victoria was writing to Lord Campbell, then Lord Chancellor:

> The Queen wishes to ask the Lord Chancellor whether no steps can be taken to prevent the present publicity of the proceedings before the new Divorce Court. These cases, which must necessarily increase when the new law becomes more and more known, fill now almost daily a large proportion of the newspapers, and are of so scandalous a character that it makes it almost

impossible for a paper to be trusted in the hands of a young lady or boy. None of the worst French novels from which careful parents would try to protect their children can be as bad as what is daily brought and laid upon the breakfast-table of every educated family in England, and its effect must be most pernicious to the public morals of the country.

It so happened that there was a series of cases over the last three decades of the century which would have appeared sensational even to our more surfeited appetites. On 26 February 1870 the *Spectator* reported:

> Town has been interested and disgusted all the week with the great 'Warwickshire Scandal', the Mordaunt Divorce case. Lady Mordaunt, wife of Sir Charles Mordaunt, daughter of Sir T. Moncreiffe, and connected with endless aristocratic houses, confessed to her husband, just after the birth of her child, that she had been 'wicked' with many men, including the Prince of Wales, Lord Cole, Sir F. Johnstone, Lord Newport, Captain Farquhar, and others, and that her child was Lord Cole's daughter. These statements were attributed by her friends to puerperal mania, but Sir Charles filed a bill for divorce. Pending the trial, Lady Mordaunt's friends affirmed that she had become mad, and that therefore no trial could be had, as she was unable to instruct attorneys. Sir Charles, on the other hand, argued that if mad now, which he denied, she was not mad when the citation was served, and he was entitled to relief. A preliminary inquiry was therefore held into the question of sanity, but as it was essential to show that Lady Mordaunt had a motive for shamming madness, this expanded into a sort of rehearsal of the divorce case. The case, owing to the number of persons accused, the Messalina character attributed to Lady Mordaunt, and the importation into it of a question of disease, was an extraordinarily disagreeable one, but it ended on Friday in a verdict of insanity.

On 23 February 1870 the Prince of Wales gave evidence. After various questions he was finally asked:

'Has there ever been any improper familiarity or criminal act between yourself and Lady Mordaunt?'

His Royal Highness (in a very firm tone): 'There has not.'

According to *The Times*: 'There was here a burst of applause which was at once repressed.' The case went on through various Courts for five years.

In August 1885 Mr. Donald Crawford, Liberal M.P. for Lanark, filed a Petition for divorce against his wife on the ground of her adultery with Sir Charles Dilke.

The Petition was heard on 12 February 1886. According to *The Times*:

> Long before the opening of the Court this morning a dense crowd of barristers and of the general public had assembled in the corridors outside, and at a few minutes past 10 o'clock, when the doors were opened, there was a rush and a scramble to secure seats, such as has rarely been seen in a court of justice. The jury box was reserved for persons who had special orders of admission, and in it the Turkish Ambassador, the Right Hon. J. Chamberlain, M.P. . . . and several others occupied seats.

The wife was found guilty of adultery and the charge against Dilke was dismissed without his having been called to give evidence. The public were not satisfied of his innocence and Dilke persuaded the Queen's Proctor to intervene with the result that there was another hearing on 16 July 1886 with yet more publicity which failed to clear Dilke's name and his political career was in ruins. Mr. Roy Jenkins, Dilke's biographer, has described the case as not only 'a personal disaster for Dilke' but also 'a major political event'.

On 4 December 1891 a Petition for judicial separation by Countess Russell against her husband was heard. The Petition was on the ground of his cruelty. In the words of the *Law Reports* she 'made allegations importing that the Earl had been guilty of an odious crime in concert with one Mr. R'. The jury acquitted the Earl of all the charges of cruelty and the Petition of the Countess was dismissed with costs. Four days later a newspaper called *The Hawk* published a statement made by the Countess to the Editor saying that she had in her possession letters to prove the charge which she had not produced at the trial.

In 1894 the Countess brought a suit for restitution of conjugal rights and the Earl asked for a judicial separation on the ground of cruelty. The case finally went to the House of Lords in 1897. It is in fact the most important case ever decided on the law of cruelty and the case of Mordaunt is also an important legal authority.

However, I am not considering these cases as authorities on points of law but as examples of cases which must have had an enormous impact on the public mind at a time when there was no radio or television but unrestricted newspaper reporting of almost every word said in Court. In each of these cases the parties were prominent, the charges sensational and the proceedings dragged on over months and years with repeated opportunities for further newspaper publicity.

Meanwhile, before the Russell case began, a Petition for divorce had been filed in another case on Christmas Eve 1889. The Petition was by a husband on the ground of his wife's adultery. It was quite a short document and in form similar to hundreds of other Petitions. It was, however, to have rather more dramatic effects than most husbands' Petitions. Here, then, is Captain O'Shea's Petition:

In the High Court of Justice

Probate Divorce and Admiralty Division

(Divorce)

To the Right Honorable the President of the said Division
The 24th day of December 1889

The Petition of William Henry O'Shea of No. 124
Victoria Street in the City of Westminster
Justice of the Peace for the County of Clare

SHEWETH

1. That your Petitioner was on the 24th day of January 1867 lawfully married to Katharine O'Shea then Katharine Wood Spinster at Saint Nicholas Church Brighton in the County of Sussex

2. That after his said marriage your Petitioner lived and cohabited with his said wife at Brighton in the said County of Sussex No. 45 Beaufort Gardens Brompton in the County of Middlesex and at Wonersh Lodge Eltham in the County of Kent and that your Petitioner and his said wife have had issue of their said marriage Six children to wit:- Gerard Henry aged 19 years, Norah Mary Katharine aged 16 years, Ana Maria Del Carmen aged 15 years, Clare Gabrielle Marcia Antoinette Esperance aged 6 years, Guadalupe Katie Flavia aged 5 years and one child a girl who died an infant in the year 1882

3. That from the year 1880 down to the filing of this Petition the said Katharine O'Shea at Wonersh Lodge Eltham aforesaid 34, York Terrace Regents Park in the County of Middlesex Woodcroft Mottingham in the County of Kent, Brighton in the County of Sussex 9 and 10 Walsingham Terrace Aldington in the said County of Sussex and at divers other places at present unknown to your Petitioner habitually committed adultery with Charles Stewart Parnell of Avondale Rathdrum in the County of Wicklow Ireland Member of Parliament.

Your Petitioner therefore Humbly Prays That your Lordship will be pleased to decree that his marriage with the said Katharine O'Shea may be dissolved
That he may have the Custody of the Children And That your Petitioner may have such further and other relief in the Premises as to your Lordship may seem meet.

William Henry O'Shea

Parnell's Answer dated 24 March 1890 was very brief and was as follows:

In the High Court of Justice
Probate Divorce and Admiralty Division
(Divorce)
O'Shea against O'Shea and Parnell

The 24th day of March 1890

Answer of the Co-Respondent

Charles Stewart Parnell the Co-Respondent by Messrs. Lewis and Lewis his Solicitors in Answer to the Petition filed herein, says:

1. That he denies that he is guilty of any or either of the acts of Adultery alleged against him.

Wherefore the Co-Respondent humbly prays that your Lordship will be pleased to reject the prayer of the said Petition.

Mrs. O'Shea's Answer dated 12 May 1890 was longer:

In the High Court of Justice
Probate Divorce and Admiralty Division
(Divorce)

12th day of May 1890

O'Shea   v   O'Shea   and   Parnell
(William Henry)   (Katharine) (Charles Stewart)

Katharine O'Shea this Respondent by Messrs. Greenfield and Cracknall Solicitors, in answer to the Petition of William Henry O'Shea filed in this Cause says as follows

1. That she denys (sic) that she committed adultery with Charles Stewart Parnell as alleged.
2. That the Petitioner was accessory to and connived at the said alleged adultery if any.
3. That the Petitioner was guilty of such wilful neglect and misconduct as has conduced to the said alleged adultery if any.
4. That the Petitioner wilfully separated himself from this Respondent before the alleged adultery complained of without reasonable excuse.
5. That the Petitioner has during the marriage been guilty of adultery with divers women in London and other places.
6. That the Petitioner has been guilty of unreasonable delay in presenting his said Petition.
7. That the Petitioner has been guilty of cruelty to the Respondent.

Wherefore this Respondent prays that your Lordship will please to reject the Prayer of the Petitioner.

Katharine O'Shea.

Both O'Shea and his wife gave further details of their respective charges. O'Shea gave particular occasions when and places where he alleged adultery had taken place. Mrs. O'Shea's further details were lengthy and they are set out in Appendix B. Amongst other charges she alleged that her husband had committed adultery with her sister Mrs. Steel. On 24 May 1890 O'Shea filed a Reply denying his wife's charges.

It is outside the scope of this book to discuss the effect of this divorce on English and Irish politics but probably no other divorce has had greater political consequences, ironically enough again involving Gladstone, who had already been affected by the Dilke case and who had so strongly opposed the 1857 Act. His role in the Parnell case was still being discussed in a libel action thirty years after his death. It is relevant to the history of divorce as the supreme example of the publicity which divorce attracted and the consequences for Parnell are a part of the history of changing public attitudes to divorce to which I refer later. But there are other aspects of the case which are worth noticing. Parnell was not represented at the hearing and Mrs. O'Shea's counter-charges were not proceeded with, her Counsel saying that he would take no part in the proceedings. O'Shea was claiming custody of the children including the two youngest girls Clare and Katie. At the trial on 15 and 17 November 1890 O'Shea was represented by the Solicitor-General who made a long opening speech rejecting the allegations of connivance which had been made. Evidence was given of Parnell's long association with Mrs. O'Shea at Eltham and elsewhere. Parnell's horses had been stabled at Eltham since 1885. Two of the horses were named President and Dictator. There was a third horse of whom the Solicitor-General was reported in *The Times* as saying:

> They were followed in the early part of 1886 by another horse called Home Rule (Laughter). This horse is described in one of the proofs before me as an old crock, and only fit to go in the shafts (Laughter). What has become of that horse I do not know (Loud Laughter).

There was also laughter while evidence was being given of an occasion in Brighton when Parnell had been with Mrs. O'Shea and O'Shea had arrived at the house. It was said that Parnell had made his escape from the drawing room by the balcony and ten minutes later had rung the front door bell and asked to see Captain O'Shea.

There may have been laughter in Court—there was not much laughter in future Anglo-Irish relations.

The allegations of connivance were rejected and O'Shea obtained a decree and also custody of Clare and Katie.

In a leader next day which alluded to the fate of Dilke *The Times* called for the head of the quarry it had so long pursued.

> The popular standard of morality may not be too exalted, but even the least prudish draw the line for public men above the level of a scandalous exposure like this, and cynically observe that, when the man of loose life is found out, he must take the consequences.

The two girls whose custody was given to O'Shea were the daughters of Mrs. O'Shea and Parnell as was the daughter who had died in infancy in 1882. Why did O'Shea claim their custody? And why if they were not his children did he get their custody? Why did O'Shea not bring a Petition earlier? Why did not his wife proceed with her cross-charges? R. C. K. Ensor writes that Parnell's

relation to Mrs. O'Shea seemed to the public in 1890 to reflect much more gravely on his character than it really did, since only O'Shea's version of it was heard in the divorce court. The incriminated pair durst not reply, because, once O'Shea had brought his action, their sole chance ever to be free from him was that he should succeed. And in order that he should, it became necessary for him to make out that he had been 'deceived' during a period of no less than nine years. It was this unmerited imputation of special and prolonged duplicity, quite as much as that of immorality, which damned Parnell with the English non conformists.

As Counsel for Mrs. O'Shea took no part in the trial, it was left to two of the jury to ask one or two questions, which showed that despite, or perhaps because of, Captain O'Shea's evidence they were not wholly satisfied on the issue raised by Mrs. O'Shea's counter-charges. And on the custody point Ensor writes:

O'Shea, having for about twenty years lived on money obtained from his wife, had by then become, in effect, a blackmailer. He could have been bought off and divorced for £20,000 . . . the money was not forthcoming, and O'Shea brought his divorce suit. One result of it was to give him the legal right of custody over Parnell's two surviving daughters, who had been born while the O'Shea coverture lasted. This was a whip-hand which he used even after Parnell's death to extort both money and silence from the widow.

In June 1891 Mrs. O'Shea and Parnell married. On 6 October 1891 Parnell died. Eighteen months later on 28 March 1893 another Order was made in the High Court. The Order dealt with a settlement dated 11 January 1867, that is a fortnight before the marriage between O'Shea and his wife. As a result of the Court's Order O'Shea received a lump sum of £6,000 and Mrs. O'Shea got the custody of Clare and Katie. In the state of the law as it then was the two girls were either the legitimate daughters of O'Shea or they were for ever illegitimate—the matter could not be put right by Mrs. O'Shea's marriage to Parnell.

By the end of the nineteenth century, therefore, divorce was a subject well in the public mind. Meanwhile, dissatisfaction with the state of the divorce laws was growing. The birth rate was falling, the movement for women's rights was gathering force, the Church's doctrine on marriage (and it was by no means certain what that doctrine was) was no longer regarded as a subject not fit for debate. With other opponents of the 1857 changes Gladstone had foretold the inevitability of further changes: 'In making a change in the law upon a subject of such importance,' he asked in the House of Commons on 24 July 1857 'what prospect is there of any stability under the new system then proposed?'

In 1883 in an article in the *Fortnightly Review* one of the most experienced contemporary divorce solicitors, Sir George Lewis, whose firm had been concerned in the Dilke, Parnell and Russell cases, urged that the law should be amended so that a divorce could be obtained on the grounds of desertion, cruelty, lunacy and imprisonment for five years as well as for adultery and that the grounds should be the same for husband and wife.

By 1890, there were 50,000 women in nursing and 150,000 in teaching. The first women's trade union had been founded in 1875 and 'it included dressmakers, upholsterers, bookbinders, artificial-flower makers, feather dressers, tobacco, jam and pickle workers, shop assistants and typists'. In 1891 the Court decided that a husband had no right to lock up his wife to prevent her from leaving him.

In November 1895 the full version of *Jude the Obscure* was published, 'the marriage laws', according to Hardy himself, 'being used in great part as the tragic machinery of the tale...'. Writing of Jude's wedding he says:

> And so, standing before the aforesaid officiator [the parson], the two swore that at every other time of their lives till death took them, they would assuredly believe, feel and desire precisely as they had believed, felt and desired during the few preceding weeks. What was as remarkable as the undertaking itself was the fact that nobody seemed at all surprised at what they swore.

And of the time not much later when Jude had been left by his wife Hardy wrote:

> Their lives were ruined, he thought; ruined by the fundamental error of their matrimonial union: that of having based a permanent contract on a temporary feeling which had no necessary connection with affinities that alone render a life-long comradeship tolerable.

Hardy also referred to legal marriage as a 'hopelessly vulgar' institution and the whole book was an attack on respectable middle-class attitudes to marriage. It was an outrage to such attitudes just because it questioned and presumed to discuss matters then taken for granted.

As a result of the publication of *Jude the Obscure* there was an outcry against Hardy from critics and clergy. Hardy decided never to write another novel and 20,000 copies had been printed within three months of publication.

In a postscript to his Preface, written in April 1912, he said:

> I have been charged since 1895 with a large responsibility in this country for the present 'shop-soiled' condition of the marriage theme. . . I do not know. My opinion at that time, if I remember rightly, was what it is now, that a marriage should be dissolvable as soon as it becomes a cruelty to either of the parties—being then essentially and morally no marriage.

Lecky had also pleaded for reform. By 1908 the big guns of George Bernard Shaw were beginning to bear on the theme. The social climate had changed with the accession of Edward VII.

Meanwhile, the President of the Probate Divorce and Admiralty Division from 1905 to 1909 had been Sir Gorell Barnes, later Lord Gorell.

On 8 November 1909 the Royal Commission on Divorce and Matrimonial Causes was appointed—largely due to Lord Gorell's strongly expressed criticism in Court and in the House of Lords of the existing state of the law in its denial of access to the Courts by poor persons. He himself was made Chairman. On 2 November 1912 it made two reports—majority and minority. Lord Gorell died six months later. Its members included the then Archbishop of York—Cosmo Gordon Lang, later Archbishop of Canterbury from 1928 to 1942, Sir William

Anson, Rufus Isaacs—later Lord Reading, Lord Derby, and J. A. Spender. It held seventy-one sittings and examined two hundred and forty-six witnesses. Its report and the evidence weigh approximately twelve pounds and total approximately one and a half million words. Among the witnesses examined were three High Court judges, eight County Court judges, thirteen Metropolitan Police and stipendiary magistrates, the King's Proctor, barristers including Sir Edward Carson, Sir Edward Clarke and Sir Frederick Pollock, solicitors and Law Societies, Scottish, Irish, Colonial and foreign judges and lawyers, bishops and clergy including Dean Inge, representatives of the Press including C. P. Scott, W. T. Stead and J. St. Loe Strachey, lunacy commissioners, prison officials, doctors, representatives of the Mothers' Union, the Divorce Law Reform Union, the N.S.P.C.C. and three gentlemen classified under the heading of 'Inebriety Experts'.

The Commission seem to have been well justified in their view that 'a full inquiry, such as has taken place before us, does not appear to have been held at any time previously in this country, nor, so far as we are aware, in any other'.

Having given an historical introduction and set out what the law as to divorce was in other countries of the world the Majority Report then dealt with the religious question. It said: 'The main ground urged by those who objected to any extension of the grounds for divorce proceedings was that such extension would be contrary to Christian principles.' The Majority did not feel it desirable to 'express any definite opinion as to what are the true Christian principles applicable to this subject'. It pointed out that 'opinions of persons equally learned, equally able, equally pious and honest, equally disinterested and humane, and equally public spirited, have differed and still differ upon the point, although the original materials upon which the differing opinions are formed are of a limited character.' The Majority went on to say:

> In the evidence given before us, opinions were maintained in favour of each of the following principles:—
>> That all marriages are indissoluble.
>> That Christian marriages are indissoluble.
>> That marriage is dissoluble on the ground of
>> adultery only.

That marriage is dissoluble on the grounds of
    (1) adultery or
    (2) desertion.
That marriage is dissoluble on other serious grounds based
upon the necessities of human life.

They noticed that with few exceptions the lay witnesses ignored the differing views of the theologians and they concluded:

> In view of the conflict of opinion which has existed in all ages and in all branches of the Christian Church, among scholars and divines equally qualified to judge, and the fact that the state must deal with all its citizens, whether Christian, nominally Christian, or non-Christian, our conclusion is that we must proceed to recommend the Legislature to act upon an unfettered consideration of what is best for the interest of the state, society, and morality, and for that of parties to suits and their families.

The Minority, which included the Archbishop of York, in their Report while agreeing that the State had to legislate for non-Christian as well as Christian said that all the representatives of the Churches had agreed 'that Christ intended to proclaim the great principle that marriage ought to be indissoluble'. Adultery, they thought, could be distinguished from other grounds because 'it breaks the tie of married life in a sense and with a completeness which can be predicated of no other wrongdoing. For the peculiarity of adultery is that it is a wilful and deliberate transfer to another person of all that is involved in the physical union of husband and wife, which has universally been regarded as the completion and consummation of marriage.'

The Majority summarized their recommendations as follows:

(1) The decentralization of sittings for the hearing of divorce and matrimonial cases to an extent sufficient to enable persons of limited means to have their cases heard by the High Court locally.

(2) The abolition of the powers of Courts of Summary Jurisdiction to make orders for the permanent separation of married persons and the introduction of amendments with regard to their powers, procedure, and practice.

73

(3) The placing of men and women on an equal footing with regard to grounds for divorce.

(4) The addition of five grounds for divorce which are generally recognized as in fact putting an end to married life.

(5) The addition of grounds for obtaining decrees of nullity of marriage in certain cases of unfitness for marriage.

(6) The introduction of other amendments of the present law, procedure, and practice in a number of details.

(7) The making of certain provisions with regard to the publication of reports of divorce and matrimonial cases.

(8) The extension of the protecting clauses in the Act of 1857 with regard to the position of the clergy of the Church of England, if the further grounds for divorce above recommended be added.

The two sexes were to be placed on an equal footing as regards the grounds on which divorce might be obtained and the grounds were to be adultery, desertion for three years and upwards, cruelty, incurable insanity after five years' confinement, habitual drunkenness found incurable after three years from first order of separation, and imprisonment under commuted death sentence. Under certain conditions a party was to be able to obtain a decree of nullity if at the time of the marriage the other party was of unsound mind or in a state of incipient mental unsoundness which became definite within six months of marriage or was subject to epilepsy or to recurrent insanity and the fact was concealed, or was suffering from venereal disease in a communicable form or, if a woman, was pregnant by another man and the pregnancy had been concealed from the husband.

The Times, which had welcomed the 1857 Act, preferred the Minority Report. 'There is', it said in a leader on 12 November 1912, 'no halfway house between marriage indissoluble except for adultery and marriage dissoluble at pleasure.' Next day in a special supplement it published the Minority Report in full. The *Spectator* took the same line. The *Manchester Guardian* was favourable to the Majority Report. The Bishop of Hull said that it might be necessary frankly to regard England as no longer a Christian country and therefore to alter the law for the sake of those who were not Christians but pagans. They were face to face with an eruption of pagan morality, and he knew that their choice would be on the side of purity and for playing the man. The Archbishop of York refused to be interviewed by the Press.

In the words of the Report of the next Royal Commission on Marriage and Divorce of 1951–5, referred to as the Morton Commission after the name of its Chairman:

> A quarter of a century was to elapse before any one of the main recommendations of the Gorell Commission for the introduction of additional grounds of divorce was given legislative effect. Between 1912 and 1937 unsuccessful attempts to implement various recommendations of the Commission were made by Lord Gorell (son of the Chairman of the Commission), Lord Buckmaster and Mr. Holford Knight, M.P. The first World War intervened to prevent any early action on the Report. In the immediate post-war years, a major social issue on which public attention was focussed was the removal of women's disabilities, and this was reflected in the sphere of matrimonial law by the passage in 1923 of an Act (sponsored by Lord Buckmaster) which empowered a wife to present a petition for divorce on the ground of adultery (without more) by her husband.

From 1923 until after the 1937 Act adultery alone was enough for wife as well as husband. The suffragette movement which had already achieved votes for women at the age of thirty had produced another small but significant fruit. As those impressive women fought on many fronts against the various bastions of male reaction their refrain, if they had known Annie of *Annie Get Your Gun* fame, might well have been:

> Anything men may have we will have also,
> We will have anything men may have too—
> No you shan't, yes we will, yes we will.

Winifred Dartie would no longer have had to go through the abortive fiasco of a suit for restitution of conjugal rights. With evidence of Monty's adultery she could have gone straight for a decree of divorce.

Before passing on we might note that two of the grounds for divorce which were recommended by the Gorell Commission and which were in A. P. Herbert's 1936 Bill but were dropped, namely, habitual drunkenness and imprisonment under commuted death sentence, are still not grounds, although with the abolition of the death penalty the latter might well have been a ground which could have been brought in by now. Habitual drunkenness which is a ground for an order in a Magistrates' Court can sometimes be used to obtain a divorce under the guise of cruelty.

Let us return now to the late twenties and early thirties when adultery was the sole ground for divorce and husbands and wives were in the same position. In the period 1926–30 the average annual number of Petitions for dissolution and nullity had risen to 4,052 and in the period 1931–5 the figure had risen to 4,784.

If your spouse had committed adultery and you had the evidence you could get a decree in an undefended suit without difficulty, subject to such comparatively minor snags as discretion, delay, condonation, connivance and collusion which we will come to later.

If your spouse had committed adultery—but what is adultery? It may seem a little late in this book to define so simple a concept and one with which everyone is familiar but the following passage from Mr. Justice Megarry's *Miscellany at Law* shows that there is by no means universal certainty on the subject:

> . . . in one case (in 1948) a petitioner for divorce stated that she understood that adultery meant illicit sexual connection between two unmarried persons with the consequent production of a child, and that without a child there could be no adultery. Other instances of ignorance which have come to the attention of the King's Proctor were said to be 'I did not think it was adultery during the daytime'; 'I thought it meant getting a girl into trouble'; and 'I thought it meant drinking with men in public houses'. And it has been averred from the bench that there are reasonably well-educated and well-informed business men of forty and upwards who honestly thought and said that 'Adultery is having sexual connection with a woman not your wife, who is not over fifty years of age; and it is not adultery if she is over fifty.'

So far as the law is concerned 'for the purposes of relief in the matrimonial jurisdiction adultery means consensual sexual intercourse during the subsistence of the marriage between one spouse and a person of the opposite sex not the other spouse . . . one act of adultery is sufficient. When mutual sexual intercourse is proved to have taken place between the respondent and someone other than the petitioner, that intercourse is deemed to have been consensual, and it is for the respondent to show that it was not so' (Halsbury's *Laws of England*, Vol. 12, p. 235).

So if a wife is raped by another man, it is not adultery but it is not necessary to constitute adultery as a ground for divorce that the penetration of the woman by the man should constitute a complete act of intercourse. If a man and woman are found in a compromising situation, in some state of undress and enjoying an impassioned embrace, they may still be able to convince a judge that they have not committed adultery in law, however much they may have done so in their hearts. If on the other hand the judge finds that they have committed adultery when in fact they had not actually yet gone so far as the legal definition they do not perhaps have much cause for complaint.

But this is leading us on to questions of evidence or proving the adultery.

There seems to be an impression amongst the general public that in many cases a faked case of adultery is presented to the Court often in the so-called 'hotel cases'. I must say that is not my impression. I am usually convinced that my client believes that adultery has been committed and I am usually convinced that my client is right. It does not seem to me altogether odd that quite a lot of adultery is committed in hotels, since they are establishments offering a private bedroom and cannot be expected to cross-examine prospective clients as to their marital status. The difficulty in most cases is not that adultery has not been committed but that by the time the wife or husband is on the trail the scent has gone cold and the hotel maid has taken in so many early morning teas to so many couples in the same room that she cannot possibly remember faces or identify a photograph—unless perhaps she has been given an especially large tip to remember or to forget. Even if she might have remembered she may have left the job, having been a university student taking a temporary job in the vacation or a young foreign girl who has long since returned to Holland, Spain or Italy.

But what about these women whose profession it is to accompany husbands to hotels for the night in return for payment, to sleep in separate single beds or well on one side of a double bed but to appear suitably unclad when the maid arrives with the early morning tea, looking as though they had had an uninterrupted eight hours of enjoyable but exhausting sexual intercourse? Do they exist in large numbers? What is the rate of pay? Is there a directory of their names and addresses? Just occasionally a rather shy husband has told me that his marriage is at an end and has hinted that he would like to avail himself of these services, not having anyone immediately available with whom he can commit adultery. I have to tell him that I don't know and that even if I did know I couldn't act in such a case.

I am glad to see that the Law Commission in their report to the Lord Chancellor, Lord Gardiner, in November 1966 on *Reform of the Grounds of Divorce, The Field of Choice* say that: 'In recent years the bogus 'hotel case' described by Sir Alan Herbert and Mr. C. P. Harvey, Q.C., has become far less common.' As Sir Jocelyn Simon pointed out in 1965:

> . . . it should at last be accepted that the professional woman named who sits up all night playing cards with the husband in a hotel bedroom to provide spurious evidence for a divorce is a literary stereotype. Under half of the divorces granted annually are on the grounds of adultery. Of these, over half are by husbands against wives; and of those by wives only a minute proportion are 'hotel' cases. In the overwhelming number of cases of adultery the spouse charged is proved to have thrown his or her lot in decisively with the person named in the petition as co-adulterer.

Even in the comparatively insignificant number of faked hotel cases which may slip through the judicial net it is almost certain that in most cases adultery will have been committed with someone even if not with the woman at the hotel. In other words the Court is being deceived as to the identity of one of the partners to the adultery but is not being deceived as to the fact of adultery having taken place. Even in this liberal age there are many people who would prefer not to disclose the identity of the woman with whom they have committed adultery. The affair may be over and the man and woman have lost touch with each other. The woman may have since married and would not welcome a Petition arriving on the breakfast table. The woman may already have been married and still be living with her husband. The man may be going to marry the woman and neither of them wants the parents to know they have been committing adultery. The man may feel that because a woman has agreed to go to bed with him she should not necessarily have her name brought into Court proceedings.

Perhaps there were more faked hotel cases in the twenties and thirties when it was not unknown where a husband and wife found life together no longer tolerable for the husband to be 'a gentleman' and take on the role of guilty party by providing evidence of his adultery. Even in Halsbury's *Laws of England* (3rd Edition, Vol. 12, p. 238) the following passage occurs:

> The Court looks with suspicion on cases where the only evidence of adultery amounts to a stay in a hotel by the respondent and an unknown person of the opposite sex. Where there is no background of an adulterous association, the Court is not always prepared to make a finding of adultery where a hotel bill is produced and a witness from the hotel is called to say that two people were in a bedroom together.

Usually, however, there is a 'background of an adulterous association' and today, provided that there is such a background, the Court will usually accept a confession statement made after warning to an Inquiry Agent often in the presence of the solicitor of the person making the confession. Usually the adulterous husband or wife is already living with the other woman or man.

I am quite sure that if I persuaded a woman to go away with me for the week-end we would run into someone who knew her, or my wife and myself, and yet in twenty years I have only known one case in which a wife discovered her husband's adultery because the husband had been spotted at an hotel with his girlfriend by a friend of his wife—and there the husband decided to confess before he was reported to his wife. Usually adultery is either successfully concealed—and for this purpose some occupations clearly have a marked advantage over others—or it is revealed by confession. Sometimes it is only suspected. Occasionally spouses find incriminating letters but they usually only start looking in handbags and suit pockets when suspicion has already been aroused by a decline in conjugal affection.

Where there is a suspicion of adultery, proof can sometimes be very difficult to obtain, especially in the not uncommon case of a husband who is fond of his wife or home comforts or both but likes some variety as well. If the husband has a convincing reason for not working from 9 a.m. to 5.30 p.m. or is one whose work takes him away from home and if he is careful to commit his adultery in a large block of flats with several entrances, in a big town, and does not stay all night, it can take many man-hours and hundreds of pounds worth of expense to produce the necessary evidence—especially in a defended case. At the stage when the wife is trying to get the evidence, she does not know whether or not—if she does get it—her husband will defend, so the money has to be spent. Nowadays the social climate towards adultery has changed from Victoria's reign to such an extent that the mere fact that a party has gone to the expense of defending an allegation of adultery influenced the Court in a recent case to find that no adultery had been committed. Who would go to the bother and expense of fighting a divorce Petition and denying such a trivial thing as an allegation of adultery, unless he or she felt very deeply about being falsely accused—such was the reasoning which influenced the Court.

Let us suppose that, in say, 1930 a wife had obtained evidence of her husband's adultery and that she decided to present a Petition to the Court; the document would have looked like this:

In the High Court of Justice,
Probate, Divorce and Admiralty Division. (Divorce.)
To the Right Honourable the President.
The 10th day of January, 1930.
The petition of Clara Delta

SHOWETH:

1. That on the 1st day of March, 1924, your petitioner, then Clara Sigma, spinster, was lawfully married to Adam Delta (hereinafter called the respondent) at the Parish Church of Loombe in the County of Wessex.

2. That after the said marriage your petitioner and the respondent lived and cohabited at divers places and at 'Redcastle', Loombe aforesaid and there is issue of said marriage now living one child namely Eva Delta born on the 2nd day of May, 1926.

3. That your petitioner is now living at 'Hazeldene' Bathbury in the county of Nouthampton, that the respondent, who is a company promoter, is now living at 'Redcastle', Loombe aforesaid, and that both your petitioner and the respondent are domiciled in England.

4. That there have been no previous proceedings in this honourable Court with reference to your petitioner's said marriage either by or on behalf of your petitioner or the respondent.

5. That the respondent has frequently committed adultery with Kate Lambda.

6. That from the month of August, 1928, until the date of this petition, at 'Redcastle', Loombe aforesaid, the respondent has lived and cohabited and habitually committed adultery with the said Kate Lambda.

Your petitioner therefore prays that in the excercise of your Lordship's discretion your Lordship will decree:

1. That her said marriage be dissolved.
2. That she may have the custody of her said child; and
3. That she may have such further and other relief as may be just.

(Signed) Clara Delta.

In this particular case the wife was asking for the exercise of the Court's discretion in her favour. This means that she herself had committed adultery, i.e. had had sexual intercourse with a man other than her husband during the marriage. It also means that even though she proved that her husband had committed adultery she was not herself entitled as of right to a decree. Whether or not she would get one was at the 'discretion' of the Court. Like every other Petitioner or Crosspetitioner, she was under a duty to disclose to the Court the fact that she had committed adultery and her solicitor was under a duty to the Court to ask her, not once and not twice, but again and again and again. For instance in a case in 1969 (*Pearson* v. *Pearson*, [1969] 1 W.L.R. 722), Mr. Justice Latey said that there should be an invariable duty on a solicitor when first taking instructions (a) to ask the client whether he or she had committed adultery, making sure that he or she understood what adultery was and (b) to advise him or her of the duty to disclose any adultery which he or she might commit later and of the possible consequences of non-disclosure. The judge went on to say that save in very exceptional circumstances, which he did not specify, the solicitor must renew his inquiry on or very shortly before the day of hearing, which is hardly calculated to endear him to a nervous client. On this case the *Law Guardian* (September 1969) commented:

> But surely there are easier ways of eliciting [the facts] than by requiring a solicitor to go on asking embarrassingly difficult questions of his client up to the very day of the trial? . . . The Court itself could be required to ask the parties if there is anything further to be disclosed. . . .

The Petitioner's own adultery was set out in a document known as a Discretion Statement usually prepared by a barrister or solicitor. If someone had committed adultery often with different people, each occasion had to be set out with the date, place, and name of the party with whom adultery had been committed. It is obvious that a barrister or solicitor who drafted a Discretion Statement could only put into it what he was told by his client. If the client was prepared to lie about his or her adultery, the full facts would not be before the Court. There was, therefore, a temptation towards dishonesty.

The principles on which the Court acted in the exercise of its discretion, varied from time to time. In the twenties and thirties it could be a serious hurdle to surmount. More recently, if a Petitioner fully disclosed his adultery in his Discretion Statement, in the words of the Law Commission in 1966: 'the Court will nearly always exercise its discretion in his favour. Refusal is normally due not to the petitioner's adultery but because it is discovered that he has failed fully to disclose it; and even such non-disclosure is often overlooked if the Court is satisfied that a full disclosure has finally been made. Obviously the undisclosed adultery of the petitioner is unlikely to be discovered unless it is still continuing or is very recent. Despite this, discretion is asked for and some acts of adultery are disclosed in about thirty per cent of all cases.' In 1965 fifty-four interventions by the Queen's Proctor were heard and allowed, but discretion was exercised in thirty-four of these.

In 1943 in the case of *Blunt* v. *Blunt*, [1943] A.C. 517, the House of Lords set out five considerations which the Court should have in mind when exercising its discretion, namely:

(1) The position and interests of any children of the marriage.

(2) The interests of the parties with whom the petitioner has been guilty of misconduct, with special regard to the prospects of their future marriage.

(3) The question whether on the withholding of a decree, there is a prospect of a reconciliation between husband and wife.

(4) The interest of the petitioner, and in particular, the interest that the petitioner should be able to remarry and lead a respectable life.

(5) The interests of the community at large, to be judged by maintaining a true balance between respect for the binding sanctity of marriage and the social considerations which make it contrary to public policy to insist on the maintenance of a union which has utterly broken down.

By 1965 the factors which the Court should take into account in deciding how to exercise its discretion were elaborated as follows (*Bull* v. *Bull*, [1968] P. 618):

[They] . . . fall into three categories. First factors relating to the interest of the persons directly or indirectly affected by the suit; those are (i) whether, if the marriage is not dissolved, there is a reasonable prospect of reconciliation between the petitioner and the respondent. (ii) The position and interest of any children of the marriage. (iii) The interest of the party with whom the petitioner has been guilty of adultery with special regard to their remarriage. (iv) The interest of the petitioner and in particular the interest that the petitioner should be able to remarry and live respectably. (v) The interest of any children born of the adulterous connection between the petitioner and the person with whom he or she committed adultery. (vi) The interest of any children born of any adulterous connection formed by the respondent.

Secondly, all other relevant factors relating to the married life of the parties. (vii) Was the petitioner or respondent the more responsible for the break-up of their marriage? (viii) What was the nature of the misconduct which necessitates the prayer for discretionary relief and were there mitigating or aggravating circumstances? (ix) Was the party seeking discretionary relief partly, and if so to what extent, responsible for the break-up of any other marriage? (x) What was the general conduct otherwise of the party seeking discretionary relief; for example, his or her conduct towards the children? (xi) On the successful intervention of the Queen's Proctor would the Court have been likely to have exercised discretion in favour of the party seeking discretionary relief if the facts finally established had been before it on the original hearing?

Thirdly, factors which may be summed up in the statement that it is in the public interest that matrimonial relief should be granted on the basis of complete candour and truthfulness on the part of the party seeking relief, these are: (xii) What were the reasons for the original or indeed any subsequent non-disclosure of adultery by the party seeking discretionary relief? (xiii) Was there perjury, that is, a false statement on oath known to be false in the original proceedings on the part of the party seeking discretionary relief? (xiv) Was the party seeking discretionary relief frank when first or subsequently questioned about the adultery and non-disclosure? (xv) Is the Court finally satisfied that it has been told the whole truth by the party seeking discretionary relief? or (xvi) Is the court satisfied that adultery or further adultery has been committed as to which a denial on oath has been maintained? (xvii) Scrutiny and determination by the Court of the 'quality' of its own judgment as to whether adultery has been committed.

It all looks rather complicated. By 1966 the position had been reached where the Law Commission could say:

'The court's task in cases in which it is asked to exercise its discretion is an embarrassing one which frequently has to be carried out without sufficient information. The discretion of the court . . . is almost invariably exercised in favour of the petitioner and it may be questioned whether it is in the public interest to refuse to grant a decree on the sole ground (i.e. in the absence of hardship to the respondent or the children) that the petitioner has blatantly disregarded his matrimonial obligations' and they referred to a particular case in 1966 'where the results of refusal to exercise discretion on the ground that the petitioner had shown a complete disregard for the sanctity of marriage were that two new stable unions formed by the parties (one of which had already resulted in the birth of an illegitimate child) could not be regularised'.

In blunter language, by the time the Divorce Reform Act of 1969 came into force, the process of asking for the exercise of the Court's discretion had become almost a farce. It tended to favour the liar at the expense of the honest; it presented the Court in practice with a very narrow discretion but one which, if not exercised in favour of the Petitioner, could do more harm than good and it imposed on solicitors the distasteful task of repeatedly cross-examining their own clients about their sexual activities—questions which could be particularly insulting to a middle-aged woman who had remained faithful to her husband throughout the marriage only to find he went off with another woman.

On the other hand, why should a wife, say, who has herself committed adultery before her husband which she has success-fully concealed, be entitled to a divorce against him in respect of his later adultery, and is it not reasonable that the Court should take into account the conduct of both parties before granting a decree or deciding financial matters? The problem seems insoluble and has certainly not been solved by the Divorce Reform Act 1969.

Apart from the Petitioner's own adultery there were other factors which might prevent a decree being granted. Some of these were absolute bars and some, such as the Petitioner's own adultery, discretionary. One of the discretionary bars was un-reasonable delay in presenting or prosecuting a Petition. According to Halsbury's *Laws of England* (Vol. 12, p. 308):

> The Court is not to be used as a place to which to come for redress whenever it suits a party to a marriage to do so, having in the meantime held the weapon of redress over the head of the other party to the marriage.

So in a case in 1955 a Petition on the ground of cruelty was dismissed by reason of delay of eighteen months after the last act of cruelty since the Court considered that the Petitioner's delay was due to the desire to use the threat of action as a weapon to hold over her spouse until such time as she thought suitable. At the other extreme in a case in 1953 the Court granted a decree when there had been thirty years' delay because the Petitioner had been saving for many years in order to start proceedings.

Every solicitor had to take delay into account and it could be a difficult factor to evaluate when say a wife was wondering whether there would be any permanent improvement in her husband's behaviour.

Of the absolute bars the three most important were connivance, collusion, and condonation. It is odd that these stumbling blocks in the path of the Petitioner should all begin with the same letter of the alphabet although it has been of great assistance to generations of law students when preparing for their examinations.

The bar of connivance was taken over from the Ecclesiastical Courts which refused a decree unless the Petitioner came to the Court with 'clean hands', that is the Petitioner must not have been, in the words of Halsbury, 'guilty of the corrupt intention of promoting or encouraging either the initiation or the continuance of the respondent's adultery'. It does not seem unreasonable that if a husband incites or compels his wife to earn money as a prostitute or encourages her to go to bed with another man for fun he should not be able to get a divorce on the ground of her adultery and yet under the Divorce Reform Act 1969 it is in theory possible that a husband who has encouraged his wife to commit adultery can come to the Court and say that he finds it intolerable to live with her and so get a decree. In practice the Court may not accept the husband's assertion that he finds life with the Respondent intolerable although, curiously enough, as the Act is worded, the Petitioner does not have to find life with the Respondent intolerable because of the adultery. In other words a husband may encourage his wife to commit adultery but satisfy the Court that he finds life with her intolerable for reasons other than the adultery and on the wording of the section he is entitled to the decree. Perhaps, by judicial interpretation, it may be held that the adultery complained of must be, at least in part, the reason why the Petitioner finds it intolerable to continue. But, take another example. Suppose, as has happened in these enlightened days, husband and wife go to a wife-swapping party. At the end of a convivial evening the husband goes off to bed with Mrs. X knowing that his wife is going to bed with Mr. X. Next morning husband and wife meet on amicable terms and recount to each other the pleasures and amusements of the preceding night. All is happy between them. Suppose, however, that during the next two months the husband begins to regret the whole incident because he finds that his wife is repeatedly comparing his sexual performance unfavourably with that of Mr. X. What could be more intolerable than that?

On the face of it he should be able to get a decree under the Divorce Reform Act 1969 because 'the respondent has committed adultery and the petitioner finds it intolerable to live with the respondent'—note that the test is not whether a reasonable man would in the circumstances have foreseen the possible effect on his wife's future behaviour but whether the particular Petitioner finds it intolerable to live with the Respondent. Under the law as it was before the Divorce Reform Act 1969 the husband's behaviour would clearly have been connivance and he would not have obtained a decree.

That this was a possible result of the new Act was pointed out at the Committee stage in the House of Commons by Mr. Bruce Campbell, Q.C., M.P., but his objections were voted down.

Of all the bars to divorce the one which has caused the greatest difficulty has been collusion. When I die, the word 'collusion' will be found written on my heart. While I was a young and inexperienced barrister I once received a brief in an undefended suit at Norwich. I arrived to find that there were about ten cases in the list but only one other barrister, a much older and more experienced man. In the tradition of the Bar he was very pleasant to me, marched into Court with nine briefs under his arm and not very long after marched out again with nine decrees nisi and a look on his face of a good day's work well done. Not very long after that I had been flung out on my ear because of collusion. I returned to London a lot sadder and a little wiser. It had emerged during the hearing of the Petition that there had been an agreement by the guilty respondent husband to pay his wife's costs. That was collusion, notwithstanding that adultery had been committed and that the husband would have been ordered by the Court to pay the costs in any event.

The *Concise Oxford Dictionary* defines collusion as a 'fraudulent secret understanding especially between ostensible opponents as in law suits'. That seems simple enough and fair enough. Most people would agree, I think, that an attempt to deceive the Court by pretending that adultery had been committed when it had not should prevent a decree being obtained. It was also collusion where two parties who wanted a divorce agreed that one should commit adultery in order that the other should have grounds on which to petition. So in a case in 1800 Lord Stowell defined collusion as 'an agreement between the parties for one to commit or appear to commit a fact of adultery, in order that the other may obtain a remedy at law as for a real injury'. In another case in 1913 (*Scott* v. *Scott*, [1913] P. 52) collusion was defined as 'an improper act done, or an improper refraining from doing an act, for a dishonest purpose'. Halsbury (Vol. 12, p. 300) takes it further—

'Collusion is held to exist where the initiation of a suit for dissolution of marriage is procured, or its conduct provided for by agreement or bargain, express or implied, between the parties or their agents, as, for instance, an agreement not to defend, even when the agreement is disclosed to the Court; because the Court will not be hampered in ascertaining for itself, whether there is danger of a husband or wife obtaining a divorce contrary to the justice of the case.' So 'for one spouse to ask the other to furnish evidence of adultery in order to petition for divorce is collusion if it amounts to a suggestion, acted upon, that the other should commit adultery; but it does not necessarily amount to collusion if it is merely a request for evidence of adultery already committed'—

which could lead to some fairly subtle conversational games between a husband and wife who were contemplating divorce and were aware of the law.

The result was that as soon as a spouse consulted a solicitor about the impending break-up of his or her marriage the solicitor warned the client not to have any discussions with the other spouse and the parties were prevented from trying to sort out for themselves all the hundred and one problems that arise when a home breaks up.

Another consequence was that a vast amount of money (public and private) was wasted in fighting a case to Court only to find a judge suggesting that the matter might be dealt with in a way which was satisfactory to the parties but would have amounted to collusion if suggested by the respective solicitors months earlier. In one case in my experience, for example, where thousands of pounds had been spent on obtaining evidence abroad and where there were bitterly fought cross-charges of the most unpleasant cruelty the judge suggested that the husband should allow his wife to divorce him on the ground of desertion and pay her a lump sum and costs. The husband and wife agreed and so it came about.

Such was the law as to collusion until 1963 when well-intentioned changes in the law were brought in which made things in many ways easier for the parties and their advisers but no less complicated.

The last major rock on which a Petition could founder was condonation—if the adultery had been forgiven it could not later be made the subject of an allegation in a Petition. When the wife was guilty of adultery and the husband, knowing of her adultery, had sexual intercourse with her even once he would be held to have condoned her offence. On the other hand if it was the husband who had committed adultery the mere fact that the wife, knowing of his adultery, had sexual inter-course with him on more than one occasion would not of itself necessarily amount to condonation because the Courts recognized that it was not always easy for a wife to walk straight out of the matrimonial home as soon as she discovered her husband's adultery.

Until 1963 where there had been condonation of adultery or cruelty so that the innocent spouse could not petition on the grounds of that adultery or cruelty, subsequent misbehaviour by the guilty spouse would revive the previous adultery or cruelty. The subsequent misbehaviour did not itself have to be further adultery or cruelty—but conduct sufficiently serious for the Court to regard it as a substantial breach of duty—so that a wife could petition when her husband who had com-mitted adultery, and had been found out and forgiven, was proved later on to be associating again with the other woman even though there was no firm evidence of further adultery. After 1963 condoned adultery could not be revived although the doctrine continued to apply in cruelty cases.

Meanwhile, so far as the mother's rights to the children are concerned the Guardianship of Infants Act 1925 marked an important stage. The Preamble says:

> Whereas Parliament by the Sex Disqualification, (Removal) Act 1919, and various other enactments, has sought to establish equality in law between the sexes, and it is expedient that this principle should obtain with respect to the guardianship of infants and the rights and responsibilities conferred thereby.

From then on it was expressly enacted that in any proceeding in any Court concerning the custody, upbringing or property of an infant the Court should regard 'the welfare of the infant as the first and paramount consideration'. It went on to say that the Court—

> 'shall not take into consideration whether from any other point of view the claim of the father, or any right at common law possessed by the father, in respect of such custody, upbringing, administration or application is superior to that of the mother, or the claim of the mother is superior to that of the father' and it provided that 'the mother of an infant shall have the like powers to apply to the Court in respect of any matter affecting the infant as are possessed by the father'.

Ostensibly women had at last achieved equal rights in relation to their children. In reality they had won more. The next forty years were to show that it would become increasingly difficult for a father to obtain physical custody of his children if the children were very young and the mother fought for their care and control. The mere fact that she was the guilty party in a divorce suit would certainly not deprive her of the children. More and more the Courts took the view that very young children should be with their mothers unless it could be shown that the mother was a bad mother. The fact that she had abandoned her husband and gone off with another man did not apparently affect her suitability as a mother.

5

DIVORCE AFTER A. P. HERBERT

In 1930 a book entitled *Divorce as I see it* was published. The contributors were Bertrand Russell, Fannie Hurst, H. G. Wells, Theodore Dreiser, Warwick Deeping, Rebecca West, André Maurois and Leon Feuchtwanger.

Bertrand Russell advocated that insanity, crime and dipsomania should be recognized as grounds for divorce and thought that where there were children adultery alone should not be a ground for divorce because there was often no desire to break up the home or any cessation of mutual affection (which seems to me to be good reason for not bringing a Petition rather than not making adultery a ground for divorce). He went on to say:

Where a marriage is childless the state has no interest in its permanence and it ought to be dissoluble on the application of either party.

With regard to adultery he said that public opinion regards excessive jealousy as not only justifiable but positively virtuous. He forecast:

Existing unduly severe laws can only be amended where there is a dominant political party not appealing for support to any of the Churches. This means that in English-speaking countries the most that can be hoped is the maintenance of the status quo, at any rate for many years to come. We shall be fortunate if we escape reactionary changes designed to please the Catholic Church.

H. G. Wells thought that 'In a modern state the well being of children is the only rational justification of a marriage bond.' He also said that 'for a large majority of people marriage is an institution for the protection and enforcement of individual sexual rights . . . sexual love should not be bought, sold, hired or made the subject of any contract whatever'.

With these views may be compared some of the views expressed by witnesses to the Gorell Commission twenty years earlier. Sir John Macdonnell, a Professor of Comparative Law of the University of London and a Master of the Supreme Court, said:

It seems to me that divorce by mutual consent, if such consent is long persevered in, if there is no hope of reconciliation, and if the interests of infant children are safeguarded, might be allowed, subject to certain restrictions; decrees on such grounds not to be granted during the first two or three years of married life; not to be granted in the first instance; the court ordering a separation for a period; at the end of it the court granting the divorce, if the parties are still of the same mind, if reconciliation has failed, and if they have made such reasonable provision as is in their power for infant children.

Mr. Maurice Hewlett said that 'bodily desire and spiritual intention to unite' were the essence of marriage and if a man ceased to desire his wife or desired another woman he ought to be entitled to apply for a divorce.

Miss Llewelyn Davies, the General Secretary of the Women's Co-operative Guild, said that the views of some members of her Guild were as follows:

When a man and wife agree to part, I feel it would be much better for the morals of both to grant a divorce. All our members are most emphatic that where husband and wife could not live happily together it was no real marriage, it was a life of fraud without love. Nothing but love should hold two together in this most sacred of all bonds.

She expressed the view that divorce should be granted whenever there was 'a serious desire on the part of either of the parties not to live with the other', and she explained that this would apply to the case of a man who wanted to be freed from his wife in order to live with another woman.

It is impossible to estimate what effect these views had on the climate of public opinion in the twenties and thirties. I suspect that A. P. Herbert's *Holy Deadlock* had a much greater impact. It was first published in April 1934 and had gone through a second edition by the end of the year. There were seven editions by 1948. Couched in the form of a novel it was in reality an outspoken attack on the existing state of the law and an eloquent plea for change seasoned throughout with wit and humour. As a novel it perhaps did not rank amongst the world's greatest. As part of a campaign for reform it could hardly have been more successful, and one can only wish that other law reformers would bring similar talents and zest into their efforts.

At an early stage of the book Sir Alan, speaking through the mouth of a solicitor, summed up the existing law and put the case for change as follows:

'This is going to be a difficult case,' said Mr. Boom. 'Three parties with principles, and one with a job at the B.B.C.'

John Adam looked at him, as one bewildered. 'Do you really mean,' he said, 'that what you call "intimacy" is the only way out of this mess? Supposing I go to Mary's flat and beat her—really knock her about? Wouldn't that do?'

'Not at all,' said Mr. Boom cheerfully. 'More brandy? Even persistent physical cruelty is not sufficient ground for a divorce. It would help your wife to get a judicial separation, but she would be no more free to marry Mr. Seal than she is now. If you violently knock your wife about every night the ordinary person will conclude that you have not much affection for her; but the law requires you to prove it by sleeping with another woman. For that is the only act of a husband that the law regards as really important. It would be the same if you were certified a lunatic: or became a habitual and besotted drunkard: or were sentenced for embezzlement to fourteen years' penal servitude: or were found guilty of murder but reprieved, and so let off with imprisonment for life. Such trifles mean nothing to the divorce laws of this Christian country. Adultery, misconduct, intimacy, or nothing—that's the rule. Human love, and Christian marriage, are rightly contrasted with the brutal mating of animals, which has no spiritual element, no mystical union of soul and mind. But if, as the law insists, the one thing that matters is the physical act of love, we are not, after all, so very different from "the brute beasts that have no understanding".'

A. P. Herbert was then one of the representatives of the University of Oxford in Parliament. In 1936 Mr. de la Bere, M.P., as he then was, succeeded in obtaining a place in the ballot for Private Members' Bills and decided to sponsor A. P. Herbert's Bill, which on 20 November 1936 was read for the second time. A. P. Herbert proposed to introduce the following additional grounds for divorce, all of which had been recommended by the Gorell Commission:

(1) desertion for three years and upwards
(2) cruelty
(3) incurable insanity after five years' confinement
(4) habitual drunkenness found incurable after three years from first order of separation
(5) imprisonment under commuted death sentence.

He also proposed to introduce, subject to certain conditions, additional grounds of nullity which had in substance been recommended by the Gorell Commission as follows:

(a) that the marriage has not been consummated owing to the wilful refusal of the respondent to consummate the marriage; or

(b) that either party was at the time of the marriage of unsound mind or a mental defective within the meaning of the Mental Deficiency Acts 1913 to 1927, or subject to recurrent fits of epilepsy; or

(c) that the respondent was at the time of the marriage suffering from venereal disease in a communicable form; or

(d) that the respondent was at the time of the marriage pregnant by some person other than the Petitioner.

The Bill was eventually enacted on 30 July 1937 after Sir Alan had dropped the grounds of habitual drunkenness and imprisonment under commuted death sentence. It came into effect on 1 January 1938 and so far as grounds were concerned the law remained unaltered for the next thirty-two years.

The Act also provided that in future, save in exceptional cases, no Petition could be filed until after three years from the date of the marriage so that it was no longer possible for a husband and wife to dissolve their marriage, perhaps by collusion, within a few months of the wedding ceremony. It was probably this provision which persuaded many to support the Bill who would otherwise have been deterred by a Bill which considerably extended the grounds for divorce.

Although the style of the speeches is different there is a great similarity between the arguments for and against A. P. Herbert's Bill and those used on other occasions when divorce has been debated.

> We . . . would therefore expect the coming of divorce to weaken family life; and to weaken it the more the easier divorce becomes.

One of the strongest reasons for not allowing desertion and cruelty as good causes of divorce is the ease with which they may be utilised for the dissolution of marriages of which the parties have simply grown tired, and mutually desire to make an end . . . experience in the United States emphatically confirms the reality of this danger. . . . The danger lies not merely in the risk of a misuse of law in individual cases, but in the creation of a habit of mind in the people; for there is evidently a tendency in the United States for husbands and wives and their friends in certain classes of society to see no discredit in divorce based on allegations of cruelty or desertion, while judges make no effort to detect collusion, but consider it to be their duty to facilitate divorce whenever the parties are obviously tired of one another's society . . . . Those proposals . . . would lead the nation to a downward incline on which it would be vain to expect to be able to stop halfway. It is idle to imagine that in a matter where great forces of human passion must always be pressing with all their might against whatever barriers are set up, those barriers can be permanently maintained in a position arbitrarily chosen, with no better reason to support them than the supposed condition of public opinion at the moment of their erection.

In all other countries into which relaxation of the marriage tie had been introduced, it commenced . . . by giving facility for dissolution only on the ground of adultery; but never had relaxation stopped there. Other cases of hardship had soon been suggested, until . . . for incompatibility of temper, and at last for mutual dislike, divorce had in some countries been allowed. . . .

The experience of other nations should, therefore, make them cautious before entering upon a track which would inevitably lead to that further step . . . the proposed facility for divorce . . . would be the opening of the floodgates of licence upon the hitherto blessed purity of English life.

I believe the Bill will weaken instead of strengthen the institution of marriage, lead to an increasing number of divorces and, quite obviously, expose more children than are exposed today to the dangers and the ill consequences that come from broken-up homes.

The above quotations date in order from 1969, 1912, 1856 and 1937.

Speaking for the Bill Lord Reading said:

It may be to some people a very dreadful thing that we should pass into law a provision which displaces adultery from the position of splendid isolation which it has hitherto held as a cause of divorce. It may be that we are doing a very rash and precipitate thing in allowing a husband or a wife to be divorced, not only for one single and perhaps unpremeditated act of adultery, but for persistent cruelty, for protracted desertion or incurable unsoundness of mind. If we are thought to be very precipitate or very rash it may be some comfort to reflect that four hundred years ago Archbishop Cranmer had the temerity to introduce a similar measure, the only difference being that for unsoundness of mind he substituted the much more advanced and drastic principle of 'deadly hostility between the spouses', and that if it had not been for the premature death of King Edward VI and the somewhat fiery temper of his successor, it might well be that the measure would have passed into law four centuries ago and your Lordships would not be occupied in discussing it as a revolutionary principle to-day.

In the House of Lords Cosmo Gordon Lang, Archbishop of Canterbury—who as Archbishop of York twenty-five years earlier had signed the Minority Report of the Gorell Commission—did not vote against the Bill—he abstained.

However, the opponents of A. P. Herbert's Bill did not prevail so now let's look at the position of a husband who had been deserted by his wife for years and who in 1938 could at last petition for divorce. His Petition would have looked like this:

IN THE HIGH COURT OF JUSTICE
PROBATE DIVORCE AND ADMIRALTY DIVISION
(DIVORCE)
To the HIGH COURT

The 10th day of June, 1938.

The Petition of Adam Delta showeth:—

1. That on the 1st day of March, 1921, the petitioner was lawfully married to Clara Delta, then Clara Sigma, spinster, (hereinafter called the respondent) at the Parish Church of Loombe in the County of Wessex.

2. That after the said marriage the petitioner and respondent lived and cohabited at divers places and at 14 Red Street, Loombe aforesaid and there is no issue of the said marriage now living.

3. That the petitioner is a railway guard and is now living at 14 Red Street, Loombe aforesaid, that the present address of the respondent is unknown to the petitioner and that both the petitioner and the respondent are domiciled in England.

4. That there have been no previous proceedings in this honourable Court or in a Court of Summary Jurisdiction with reference to the petitioner's said marriage either by or on behalf of the petitioner or respondent.

5. That the respondent has deserted the petitioner without cause for a period of at least three years immediately preceding the presentation of this petition.

6. That on the 4th day of April, 1924 the respondent deserted the petitioner, in that she on the said date without cause and without the consent of the petitioner withdrew from cohabitation with the petitioner at 2 Green Street, Loombe aforesaid, with the intention of bringing cohabitation between the petitioner and the respondent permanently to an end and has ever since without cause or the consent of the petitioner and with the said intention lived separate and apart from him.

The petitioner therefore prays that the discretion of the Court may be exercised in his favour and

1. That his said marriage may be dissolved
2. That he may have such further and other relief as may be just.

ADAM DELTA

You will notice that his wife left him years before, that there are no children of the marriage and that he is asking for the discretion of the Court to be exercised in his favour. Before the Petition was filed he would have seen his solicitor and told him the story—in this case sad but simple. His wife walked out on him soon after the marriage, he met another woman with whom he has been living for years and by whom he has had children and he has come along to get a decree as soon as possible after the new ground of desertion has been introduced and he has the necessary money. He may well have given to the solicitor a faded, torn, pathetic note left for him by his departing wife which he found on his return home from work to an empty house and which he has been carrying around in his wallet ever since. He will have to satisfy the Court that his wife left him without reasonable cause, that he and his wife have in fact been living apart for at least three years immediately preceding the presentation of the Petition and that discretion should be exercised in his favour. One day he will have to go to the Courts and, there, in public, stumble through his old private sorrows. But it is a simple case and in ten minutes or so he should have his decree nisi. Hundreds and thousands of such cases have gone through undefended since the 1937 Act but in the case above we have forgotten one thing. It has not been proved that the Petition has been served on the wife and unless there is proof of service or an order from the Court dispensing with service the Court will not hear his Petition. Perhaps in this case it will be all right. Although he no longer knows where she lives at present, he does know some of her family and they will let him know. But if his wife left him a long time ago and lost touch with her family and moved to a different part of the country or the world he may have to wait months and spend a lot of money while inquiries are made until eventually she is found or an order can be obtained from the Court dispensing with service or allowing service by advertisement in a newspaper. Sometimes attempts to effect service can take up to two years.

That was a straightforward undefended divorce—now let us look at a defended case in 1939 where the wife is alleging cruelty. There will be a Petition and an Answer and Cross-petition and requests for what are called Further and Better Particulars (jargon for 'more detail'). All these documents may be lengthy and I shall only give the Petition and the Answer and Cross-petition. But before I do so let us consider why the case is being fought. I think there can be five reasons. The husband may be opposed to divorce on religious grounds; he may resent being found guilty in Court of conduct of which he was not guilty; he may be spiteful, not caring whether or not the marriage is at an end but automatically opposed to a divorce because that is what his wife wants; he may be genuinely attached to the children and fear, rightly or wrongly, that if he lets the allegations of cruelty go through undefended it may be a black mark against him in any later proceedings about the children; he may be reluctant to be saddled with a liability to maintain his wife.

If it is the husband who is the Petitioner and the wife who is the Respondent the same considerations may prevail, the only difference being that on the financial side she will be fighting so as not to lose her right to maintenance. There can be no statistical support for the dogmatic assertion that in fact most defended cases are defended because of the question of maintenance but that would be the view of most lawyers. In the words of the President of the Probate Divorce and Admiralty Division in 1965:

. . . contested cases are generally disputed because of the repercussions of the offence alleged on maintenance or custody, mainly the former. There is nothing surprising or alarming about this. Whatever the basis for dissolution of marriage, it would be unjust to require a husband who had performed substantially all his matrimonial obligations to provide maintenance for a wife who had substantially repudiated hers. Similarly, where a wife has substantially performed the whole of her matrimonial obligations and the husband has repudiated his, the twin pillars of justice and humankind's division of labour require that the husband should be under a continuing obligation to support the wife. The fact that the motive for the contest relates to rights and obligations as to maintenance does not mean that the contest as to the matrimonial offence is in any sense an unreal one.

The wife's Petition in the defended case we are now considering might have looked like this:

IN THE HIGH COURT OF JUSTICE

PROBATE DIVORCE & ADMIRALTY DIVISION
(DIVORCE)

To the HIGH COURT

The 15th day of July 1939.

The petition of Clara Delta showeth:—

1. That on the 1st day of March 1927 the petitioner, then Clara Sigma, spinster, was lawfully married to Adam Delta (hereinafter called the respondent) at the Parish Church of Loombe in the County of Wessex.

2. That after the said marriage the petitioner and respondent lived and cohabited at divers places and at 'Redcastle' Loombe aforesaid and there is issue of the said marriage now

living namely Eva Delta born on the 2nd day of May 1929 and Ian Delta born on the 3rd day of March 1935.

3. That the petitioner is now living at 'Hazeldene' Bathbury in the County of Nouthampton; that the respondent, who is a company director, is now living at 'Redcastle' Loombe aforesaid, and that both the petitioner and the respondent are domiciled in England.

4. That there have been no previous proceedings in this Honourable Court or in a Court of Summary Jurisdiction with reference to the petitioner's said marriage either by or on behalf of the petitioner or respondent.

5. That the respondent has since the celebration of the said marriage treated the petitioner with cruelty.

6. That the respondent is a man of ungovernable temper and has treated the petitioner with cruelty and struck her and made married life intolerable.

7. That soon after the marriage the respondent caused the petitioner great distress by deliberately burning all records of the wedding including an album of photographs.

8. That on or about the 15th day of April 1929, shortly before the birth of the said child Eva, the respondent struck the petitioner in the face bruising her left eye.

9. That on or about the 14th day of June 1936 the respondent hit the petitioner with his fist, threw a plate at her and twisted her arm.

10. That on frequent occasions between the end of 1936 and the end of 1938 the respondent came home drunk, shouted at the petitioner, frightened the children and called the petitioner 'a lazy idle bitch who had been brought up in the gutter'. The respondent frequently vomited in the bedroom and the petitioner had to clear up the mess.

11. That on two occasions in about December 1938 the respondent hit the petitioner causing her bruising.

12. That on frequent occasions when visitors came to the home the respondent criticized the petitioner in their presence, thereby causing her embarrassment and distress.

13. That the respondent frequently said that marriage meant nothing to him and on several occasions refused marital intercourse and slept in a separate room.

14. That for long periods the respondent adopted a sullen and resentful attitude towards the petitioner, refusing to talk to her, shutting himself away from her upstairs and declining to take part in social life with her.

15. That as a result of the respondent's conduct aforesaid the petitioner's health has been seriously affected.

16. That the respondent is a company director and has an income of £3,000 per annum and upwards and is possessed of stocks and shares, a house, furniture and a motor car the value whereof is unknown to the petitioner.

The petitioner therefore prays:—

1. That her said marriage may be dissolved;
2. That she may have custody of her said children;
3. That the respondent may be condemned in the costs of this suit;
4. That the respondent do pay to the petitioner such sums by way of alimony pendente lite as the Court shall think just;
5. That she may have such further and other relief as may be just.

CLARA DELTA

In brief the husband was violent, bad tempered, sullen, selfish and drinking to excess. No one reading such a story could doubt the sufferings of the wife but what is cruelty in law?

According to Halsbury 'the legal conception of cruelty, which is not defined by statute, is generally described as conduct of such a character as to have caused danger to life, limb, or health (bodily or mental), or as to give rise to a reasonable apprehension of such danger'. The law has never been such an ass as to suppose that physical violence was the only form of cruelty. A decree will be awarded on proof of subtler methods of unkindness provided there is medical evidence of an effect on the Petitioner's health. The trouble is that it is much easier to prove bruised flesh than bruised feelings and, until the Divorce Reform Act 1969, there has always been a grave element of unfairness in the need for medical evidence in relation to non-physical cruelty. If wife A nags and scolds her husband B to such an extent that he gets nervous headaches or stomach trouble or nears the point of nervous breakdown and his doctor attributes his ill-health to his marital problems, husband B will get a decree on cruelty.

If, on the other hand, wife C nags and scolds her husband D for years to an even greater extent than does wife A but husband D grits his teeth, grins and bears it and does not go to his doctor he will not get a decree.

Writing of the costermongers, Mayhew says that one told him:

> Why, there's numbers of men leave their stock money with their women, just taking out two or three shillings to gamble with and get drunk upon. They sometimes take a little drop themselves, the women do, and get beaten by their husbands for it, and hardest beaten if the man's drunk himself. They're sometimes beaten for other things too, or for nothing at all. But they seem to like the men better for their beating them. I never could make that out.

On this point Halsbury puts it thus:

> In determining what constitutes cruelty regard must be had to the circumstances of each particular case, keeping always in view the physical and mental condition of the parties, and their character and social status.

and in a footnote adds: 'blows between parties in the lower and higher stations of life bear different aspects'.

The Minority of the Gorell Commission in their Report said:

> The conception of what constitutes cruelty differs materially in classes and even in families; it may also differ in the minds of judges. A blow in one class of life is not the unforgivable injury that it might be in another: a frankness of sarcastic speech that would be regarded as injurious to 'mental health' in one family might be the daily practice of another and regarded as an agreeable characteristic by themselves and their friends.

What would the husband's Answer and Cross-petition have looked like? Here it is, omitting the formal parts:

> 1. He is not guilty of cruelty as alleged in the said petition or at all. Save as hereinafter expressly admitted he denies each and every allegation in paragraphs 5 to 15 inclusive of the petition.
>
> 2. He admits that, as alleged in paragraph 7 of the petition, he burnt congratulatory messages received on the occasion of the wedding and the wedding photographs. He was provoked into so doing by the conduct of the petitioner who immediately prior thereto had expressed regret at ever having married the

petitioner and said that she had made a mistake in not marrying the respondent's best man at the wedding, namely Seth Beta.
3. He admits that on or about the 15th day of April 1929 he struck the petitioner in the face, as alleged in paragraph 8 of the petition. Immediately prior thereto the petitioner had said to the respondent 'how do you know it's your child?'
4. He admits that he did the acts referred to in paragraph 9 of the petition but he was provoked by the conduct of the petitioner in that she had immediately before struck him a violent blow on the head with a saucepan and called him 'a yellow-livered skunk'.
5. He denies that he has ever come home drunk or frightened the children. He admits having said, as is the case, that the petitioner was lazy and idle but denies having called her a 'bitch' or having said that she 'had been brought up in the gutter'. On a few occasions in the months of June and July 1937 he vomited in the bedroom. During the same period he was also on occasions vomiting at work. The said vomiting was not caused by drinking but by a nervous stomach condition for which the respondent was receiving medical treatment.
6. He admits having hit the respondent, as alleged in paragraph 11 of the petition. On each of the said occasions the petitioner had threatened to leave him and go off to live with the said Seth Beta.
7. He denies having criticized the respondent, as alleged in paragraph 12 of the petition.
8. He admits that on a few occasions he has slept in a separate bedroom and has shut himself away upstairs. At the time he was studying for an examination and it was only by so doing that he could free himself for study from the petitioner's continual nagging.
9. If, which is denied, the respondent has been guilty of the alleged or any cruelty, the petitioner with full knowledge of the facts alleged condoned the same by cohabiting with him until January 1939.
10. The petitioner has since the celebration of the said marriage committed adultery.
11. On the 16th April 1938 the petitioner committed adultery with the said Seth Beta at Greenacres Farm, Ullathorne, in the County of Barset.

It concluded by asking for the Petition to be dismissed and for a decree with costs against Seth Beta. The husband also asked for custody of the two children.

The first thing one feels is that either the wife or the husband is a complete liar and that the case will be decided on which of the two the judge believes in the box. But when one has read and re-read the Petition and Answer one begins to see, as is often the case, that both may be telling the truth as they remember it about the same incidents but filtered only through the memory of each and from the viewpoint of each. Indeed, each, at the time, may only have observed that part of the scene which confirmed a pre-existing opinion of the other's character and behaviour. Taken on its own and supported by medical evidence or corroboration of bruising, the wife's Petition would have succeeded without difficulty in an undefended case. But let the husband defend and the whole situation becomes confused. Who gave the blow but—who gave the provocation for the blow but—why did the one who gave the provocation want to provoke? And so one can go on desperately searching for and probably never finding the truth.

The process of probing in and out of Court takes a lot of time and therefore costs a great deal of money. Where a case of cruelty involves an almost day-by-day account of the married life the trial can take days and sometimes weeks. Even without fashionable leading Counsel the costs can amount to several thousand pounds. The trial is usually only the tip of the iceberg of work which has gone before.

In the particular case which we are now looking at both parents have claimed custody. The marriage finally broke up about a week before the Petition was filed. The husband left the matrimonial home and took with him the two children of the family. As soon as she had filed her Petition the wife applied for an order for interim custody, that is, she asked the Court to order that the children should be returned to her custody, care and control immediately. She filed an affidavit in support of her application alleging among other things that some of the husband's violent behaviour to which she had referred in her Petition had taken place in front of the children. The husband filed an affidavit in reply in which he denied the wife's accusations and made counter-accusations claiming that the wife was a bad mother who failed to look after the children properly in that she was often not at home when they returned from school, failed to cook their meals, neglected their clothing and lost her temper in front of them. Further affidavits were put in by both sides. The wife filed an affidavit by an eminent psychiatrist saying that the husband's violent behaviour was having an upsetting effect on the children one of whom had developed nervous eczema and the other of whom was still wetting his bed at a late age. The husband produced several affidavits from people who knew the family confirming that she had been a neglectful mother. The wife countered with several other affidavits by other friends who said that the children were kept pretty well and anyhow always seemed happy to be with their mother.

The application came before the judge in Chambers—that is he sat in private without wig and robes—and if I may digress to mention a particular bee that buzzes in my bonnet—he did not look any less impressive without them. A judge is a good judge because he or she is a man or woman of integrity, experience, sympathy and considerable intellectual calibre and these qualities are just as marked in an unwigged and unrobed judge, nor do wig and robes hide their lack.

No judge likes deciding custody cases or fights over care and control and access. He is anxious to do what is best for the children and to cool the heated atmosphere between the parties. He can hardly ever please both parents. He has to tread warily in a minefield of conflicting evidence. Nowadays he probably starts with the feeling that very young children should be with their mother and it usually needs very convincing evidence that she is a bad mother to displace the judge's initial tendency to let the mother have the children. In this particular case he decided that the children should be returned to the mother and their home which was near their schools. He was inclined to think that the mother was a little feckless in looking after the children but he also believed those witnesses who said that the children were happy with their mother.

Outside in the corridor after the judge's decision was known the husband was very angry and upset—he felt more affidavits should have been obtained and was all for going to the Court of Appeal. His Counsel and solicitor told him that the Court of Appeal only rarely intervened in a custody case and varied the judge's decision. The husband remained angry and became even angrier when he saw down the corridor his wife smiling triumphantly with her barrister and solicitor. A dispute about the children's future had become another round in the fight between wife and husband.

Sometimes instead of deciding the case on affidavit evidence, perhaps supplemented by oral evidence from the parents and doctors, a judge will adjourn it to get a report from a welfare officer who will go to visit the parents and their homes, hear what both have to say, chat to the children, and then make a long report to the judge which both parents see. There is only one major thing wrong with the welfare officers. There are not enough of them.

Meanwhile, with the fight for interim custody ended, pleadings are being exchanged in the main suit, witnesses being interviewed, further details of the opponent's case being sought, perhaps hundreds of letters being read and copied. Eventually after all the pleadings have been filed, parties served, and Discretion Statements put in, the Court will give directions about where the case is to be tried and the case will then join the queue of defended cases waiting to be heard. It may be months before the case comes on for hearing or it may be heard very soon—it depends on how many judges are available, how many cases are ahead in the queue but even more on how many of the cases ahead in the queue are actually contested at the hearing. In very many defended divorce cases agreements are reached and approved by the Court long before they are due to come on for hearing; in some cases agreement is arrived at outside the door of the Court and in some even after the trial has begun.

While the case is waiting to come on for trial the wife and husband are fighting about maintenance for her and the children and about access. She has obtained an order from the Court that he must pay into Court a sum of money in respect of her costs and she has started separate proceedings under the Married Women's Property Act 1882 in support of her claim to a long list of furniture items which she says she bought from her earnings before the first child was born.

It does not follow that in every case in which the Petition is defended there will also be a fight over the children, maintenance, the house and furniture. But on the whole fighting stimulates fighting so that arguments about the children may go on for years, perhaps ten or fifteen years if the children are only two or three years old when the parents part.

At last our case comes on for trial. The judge believes the wife's evidence that on two or three occasions her husband hit her with his fist and bruised her. He also thinks, but perhaps does not say, that on one occasion she deserved it. Although the wife denies that she has committed adultery the judge accepts the evidence that she and the party cited have been seen together on several occasions obviously on terms of affection and that on several occasions the party cited had called at the matrimonial home during the afternoon while the children were still at school and the husband at work. The judge grants decrees to both wife and husband. His secret opinion is that the wife is a warm-hearted, affectionate, lazy woman, a poor housewife but a cheerful and cheering mother. He thinks that the husband is very hard-working, obsessed with cleanliness, keen on getting on and making the children get on. He feels that they are an ill-assorted couple and is glad that he can end the marriage but that it is a pity that it had to be fought out.

But it had to be—because the wife was afraid that if she admitted to committing adultery during the afternoon at home she might lose the children and because the husband also thought that the charges of cruelty against him were so wrapped up with the fight about the children that it would be dangerous not to defend the charges.

Both wife and husband had obtained decrees nisi but they were not yet free to marry. In 1939 they would have had to wait six months before they could apply for their decree nisi to be made absolute unless the Court made a special order abridging the period. This period was to give the King's Proctor an opportunity to intervene if it came to his knowledge that there had been, for example, undisclosed collusion in the prosecution of the suit. This period between decree nisi and decree absolute may have played some part in the Abdication Crisis of 1936. On 27 October of that year Mrs. Simpson obtained a decree nisi at Ipswich. In December the story came out in the English Press. Writing of this incident, A. J. P. Taylor says:

[Edward VIII] bowed to Baldwin's ruling that the question should be settled quietly behind the scenes, and settled without delay. . . . There is no clear evidence why the King allowed himself to be rushed in this way. Baldwin threatened that the cabinet would resign if their advice against marriage were not accepted. It would have been difficult, indeed impossible, for them to resign if Edward had merely declined to give a promise against a hypothetical marriage at some time in the future and had then withdrawn to Windsor or Balmoral. On the other hand, ministers had a powerful weapon at hand, though there is little evidence that they threatened to use it. In the then state of English law, Mrs. Simpson's decree could not become absolute for six months. Until then it could be challenged. A law clerk called Stephenson duly 'intervened' and withdrew his intervention after Edward's abdication. Stephenson was a clerk in a firm sometimes employed by Baldwin. However, the most probable explanation is that Edward was in a hurry to get married. As part of the price for abdication he was promised a special act of parliament, making Mrs. Simpson's divorce absolute at once. At the last moment, the cabinet decided that this would have the appearance of a corrupt bargain, and the promise was not fulfilled. Edward and Mrs. Simpson did not marry until 3rd June 1937.

When the 1857 Act was passed there was only one decree and the parties were free to remarry when it was clear there would be no appeal. In 1860 an Act introduced the concept of decree nisi and decree absolute and provided that there should be a period of three months between the two. The period was increased to six months by another Act of 1866 and the period remained at six months till 1946 when it was reduced to six weeks. Following on a recommendation of the Morton Commission the period was increased to three months in 1957 and it still remains at three months, so we are back to where we were in 1860.

At present, therefore, the successful Petitioner must wait three months before applying for the decree nisi to be made absolute and if he or she does not then do so the Respondent must wait another three months before an application can be made. Most people are only too anxious to apply for the decree nisi to be made absolute as soon as possible and often have plans to remarry within a day or two of the decree nisi being made absolute. However, it is prudent for the solicitor to ask the client to confirm that he or she wants the decree nisi made absolute. Occasionally a decree nisi has been made absolute only to find that in the meantime there has been a reconciliation between husband and wife and it is not at all infrequent for a judge to be asked to rescind a decree nisi because the parties have become reconciled.

Unfortunately there was no reconciliation in the case we have been considering and after the decrees had been made absolute there remained the question of maintenance to be dealt with on a more permanent basis than during the course of the proceedings—although no maintenance order is ever final.

Once again there was a fight—affidavits were filed on both sides. The wife was suspicious that her husband had not disclosed his financial position fully. He alleged that she was capable of getting at least part-time work. She replied that it was impossible when the children were still so young. Eventually the matter would be fought out behind closed doors before one of the Registrars of the Court.

In thousands of cases these Registrars make orders of far greater importance to more men, women and children than most cases decided by High Court or County Court judges in public. An additional pound or ten shillings a week may be of the utmost importance to the payer and to the recipient when incomes are low. Even small orders multiplied over a period of years amount to substantial sums of money. In the case of wealthier husbands maintenance orders will mount to a total of thousands of pounds in a comparatively short time. Now large payments of capital can also be ordered. In February 1947 the Denning Committee reported:

> In our opinion the procedure in the Divorce Court with regard to maintenance should be entirely changed. The present procedure does not treat the issue as being so serious to the parties as it in fact is. An award of maintenance often involves considerable payments over many years, indeed for the lives of the parties. In coming to its decision the Court by statute has to have regard not only to the fortune of the wife and to the ability of the husband, but also 'to the conduct of the parties'. Such an issue should in our opinion be tried by a Judge, and not by a Registrar, and should indeed be tried by the Judge who hears the divorce suit, because

he is the person who hears the evidence as to the conduct of the parties and can better have regard to it than a Registrar who has only affidavits before him.

The recommendation was never carried out.

On what principles do the Registrars arrive at their decisions? As we have seen one of the main reasons which has led in the past to divorce Petitions becoming defended, is that the husband and wife are worried about maintenance. Naturally enough when a client goes to a solicitor one of the first questions asked is 'How much shall I get?' or 'How much shall I have to pay?' For many years solicitors have advised their clients that an innocent wife may expect to receive as maintenance for herself an amount which would bring her income, if any, together with her husband's maintenance payments, to one third of the total of the joint gross incomes of herself and her husband. So that if a wife had no income and her husband had an income of £1,200 she could expect a maintenance order for £400 per annum less tax for herself, with additional maintenance if she had to look after the children. If on the other hand she had income of her own of £300 per annum and her husband had an income of £1,200 she would only get an order for £200 per annum less tax from her husband because one third of the total of the joint gross income is £500 and she already has £300 so he would only be ordered to pay the difference of £200.

Whether this so-called one-third rule worked fairly in favour of wives is very doubtful but it had one great merit. It meant that in thousands and thousands of cases—provided there was no suspicion about the figures disclosed of the respective incomes—maintenance orders could be agreed by negotiation between solicitors and so the expense involved in a fight over maintenance at Court could be avoided. In the words of Lord Denning (*Ward* v. *James*, [1966] 1 Q.B. 273): 'Parties should be able to predict with some measure of accuracy the sum which is likely to be awarded in a particular case, for by this means cases can be settled peaceably, and not brought to Court, a thing very much to the public good.'

It is true that he was speaking of awards of damages in civil actions but the principle seems equally right in maintenance cases. From time to time some judges did emphasize that there was no such thing as the one-third rule but the profession as a whole—both barristers and solicitors—continued to apply it in practice. As recently as 1964 in a case in the Court of Appeal (*Williams* v. *Williams*, [1965] P. 125) it was said:

> The two figures of £700 for the wife and £1,088 for the husband do not look right. The wife has much more than the one third which is sometimes mentioned as a convenient proportion in maintenance applications after a divorce, although, of course, there is no rigid standard.

It is clear from this judgment that, although they were careful to emphasize that there is no rigid standard, the Court of Appeal recognized that in practice the one-third basis was followed, and implicitly approved that practice. That judgment was pronounced on 7 July 1964. One week later in another case (*Kershaw* v. *Kershaw*, [1966] P. 13) the President of the Probate Divorce and Admiralty Division, Sir Jocelyn Simon, referred to the one-third rule or one-third approach as being 'discredited' and said that in his view:

> If cohabitation is destroyed by the wrongful conduct of the husband, the wife's maintenance should be so assessed that her standard of living does not suffer more than is inherent in the circumstances of separation. . . . In general the wife should not be relegated to a lower standard of living than that which her husband enjoys.

This new principle enunciated by the President has since been followed in other cases. It is difficult to say how far it has percolated through the profession because undoubtedly many orders have since been negotiated on the basis of the one-third approach which as late as 1969 was referred to as the 'conventional test' in *Brister* v. *Brister*, [1970] 1 W.L.R. 644. What is clear, however, is that although the new principle is fairer to wives, it makes it almost impossible for legal advisers to say what the right figure should be—the right figure being what the Court will decide if the case is allowed to go to Court.

The barrister or solicitor can now only advise his client that if he or she wants to be certain there must be the expense of litigation. This tendency to do greater justice to wives—a wholly admirable one—will be given a great impetus by the Matrimonial Proceedings and Property Act 1970 which sets out the considerations to be taken into account on financial applications as follows:

5.—(1) It shall be the duty of the court in deciding whether to exercise its powers under section 2 or 4 of this Act in relation to a party to the marriage and, if so, in what manner, to have regard to all the circumstances of the case including the following matters, that is to say—

(a) the income, earning capacity, property and other financial resources which each of the parties to the marriage has or is likely to have in the foreseeable future;

(b) the financial needs, obligations and responsibilities which each of the parties to the marriage has or is likely to have in the foreseeable future;

(c) the standard of living enjoyed by the family before the breakdown of the marriage;

(d) the age of each party to the marriage and the duration of the marriage;

(e) any physical or mental disability of either of the parties to the marriage;

(f) the contributions made by each of the parties to the welfare of the family, including any contribution made by looking after the home or caring for the family;

(g) in the case of proceedings for divorce or nullity of marriage, the value to either of the parties to the marriage of any benefit (for example, a pension) which, by reason of the dissolution or annulment of the marriage, that party will lose the chance of acquiring;

and so to exercise those powers as to place the parties, so far as it is practicable and, having regard to their conduct, just to do so, in the financial position in which they would have been if the marriage had not broken down and each had properly discharged his or her financial obligations and responsibilities towards the other.

This, by the back door, will introduce the principle of Community of Property to a limited extent into English law but, in so far as it does introduce Community of Property it will benefit only those wives whose marriages end in divorce. For happily married wives there will still be no legal recognition of the contribution they make 'to the welfare of the family, including any contribution made by looking after the home or caring for the family'.

6

DIVORCE FOR ALL—FROM THE LEGAL AID AND ADVICE ACT 1949 TO 1969

But please do not imagine that the evils of indissoluble marriage can be cured by divorce laws administered on our present plan. . . . Until divorce is as cheap as marriage, marriage will remain indissoluble for all except the handful of people to whom £100 is a procurable sum.
GEORGE BERNARD SHAW: From the Preface to *Getting Married* (1908)

Whether the Bill was right or wrong, he thought it absolutely impossible, if it were carried, that legislation could stop there. When this relief was carried (if relief it were), a very active spirit of dissatisfaction would be sure to be engendered among those classes within whose reach were not brought those facilities which the Legislature would then have distinctly pronounced to be a benefit and a right as regarded the higher classes of society. Their Lordships would then be compelled to adopt some further measure to accomplish the same ends and to increase these facilities, and he really saw no limit to their legislation upon this subject until they brought the law of divorce within the jurisdiction of the County Courts, or of some other court in which justice (if justice it were) should be made still cheaper and easy of access to the very lowest classes of society. That was a prospect which he, for one, could certainly not regard with satisfaction, comfort, or confidence, and he should therefore be very glad to have an opportunity of maturely considering the provisions and effect of the measure now proposed.
THE BISHOP OF ST. DAVIDS: *Hansard*, 26 June 1856

In 1951 the Royal Commission on Marriage and Divorce was appointed under the Chairmanship of Lord Morton. Its first meeting was held on 8 October 1951 and its report was presented to Parliament in 1956. It held 102 meetings in London and Edinburgh and heard evidence from 67 organizations and 48 individuals and received a large number of memoranda and letters. It cost £35,463 4s. 6d. In an early paragraph of its report it referred to the Registrar General's remark that:

In terms of numbers, the effect of the First World War was to cause 15 *hundred* more petitions to be filed each year and of the Second World War to cause 20 *thousand* more petitions to be filed each year.

Whether the two World Wars were in themselves the sole causes of the respective increases may be doubted. As the Commission pointed out, there had been additional grounds since 1937 and the Legal Aid and Advice Act 1949 was enabling more people to petition. However, of the fact of the change in the rate of increase there can be no doubt.

The most important issue to be considered by the Commission was whether the existing divorce law should be re-framed so as to do away with the doctrine of the matrimonial offence and in future be based on the doctrine of breakdown of marriage.

Until the concept of breakdown was introduced into the English law of divorce the Petitioner had to establish a ground—the Petition had to be fitted into one of the slots marked:

Adultery
Desertion
Cruelty
Rape, sodomy or bestiality
Insanity

Provided that the facts could be made to fit into one of these grounds, that the Petition was undefended and that there were no snags over the Petitioner's own adultery, connivance, collusion, condonation or delay, then once the machine had been started, out would come, five to six months later, a decree nisi. Except for the last ground of insanity each of these grounds involved the concept of fault and so it became customary to refer to the innocent or guilty party. It is interesting to note that the grounds recommended by the Gorell Commission were regarded by the majority as causes which 'are generally and properly recognized as leading to *the break up of married life*' (the italics are mine). In 1951 in *The Reform of the Law*, edited by Glanville Williams, the Haldane Society had said:

It is therefore desirable so to alter the grounds of divorce that the law will afford legal recognition to the end of any marriage which has in fact clearly broken down and will do so at a cost which does not prevent ordinary people from exercising their legal rights.

The arguments in favour of introducing the doctrine of breakdown were summarized by the Morton Commission as follows:

[Some witnesses] recommended that the existing grounds of divorce should be abolished and their place taken by a single, comprehensive ground which would allow divorce to be granted if it could be proved that the marriage had irretrievably broken down. These witnesses argued that the matrimonial offences on which divorce is founded under the present law are not usually the real causes of the breakdown of a marriage but merely its symptoms: that the result of basing the grounds of divorce on symptoms is to deny relief where it should be available because the marriage is completely at an end, and to grant divorce (e.g. for an isolated act of adultery which had been repented of) where there is no reason why the marriage should not continue. They alleged that people deliberately commit offences, or pretend to commit them, in order to supply grounds for divorce, and suggested that the solution is to require the court to determine in each case whether the marriage has broken down beyond hope of reconciliation.

Those on the Commission in favour of the principle of breakdown said that in their view the law of divorce as it then existed was 'weighted in favour of the least scrupulous, the least honourable and the least sensitive; and that nobody who is ready to provide a ground of divorce, who is careful to avoid any suggestion of connivance or collusion and who has a co-operative spouse, has any difficulty in securing a dissolution of the marriage'. But they also thought that divorce should still be available for adultery, cruelty and desertion.

Those on the Commission who were opposed to the introduction of the principle of breakdown said that it was 'in the best interests of the community that the matrimonial offence should remain the determining principle of the divorce law'. They admitted that there was 'an element of artificiality in the doctrine of the matrimonial offence, and the consequential emphasis on legal guilt and innocence; for in real life it is comparatively rare to find all the right on one side and all the wrong on the other'. However, they thought that the doctrine of the matrimonial offence provided 'a clear and intelligible principle', and they went on to say:

> It makes for security in marriage, because husbands and wives know that they cannot be divorced unless they have committed one of the matrimonial offences which is ground for divorce. Moreover, these 'offences' are not arbitrary ones; in each case a grave injury has been done, which has cut at the root of the concept of marriage as a partnership for life.

In the event, the Commission was split over this major issue. All save one member were in favour of retaining the doctrine of the matrimonial offence. Nine members were against introducing the principle of breakdown as exemplified by divorce by consent, divorce at the option of either spouse after a period of separation or divorce on a comprehensive ground of breakdown of marriage. The other nine members recommended that:

> There should be provision for divorce in cases where quite apart from the commission of a matrimonial offence, the marriage has broken down completely; accordingly, where husband and wife have lived separate and apart for a period of at least seven years immediately preceding the application, it should be possible for either spouse to obtain a decree dissolving the marriage, *provided that the other spouse does not object* [the italics are mine].

In other words they were recommending as an additional ground for divorce—divorce by consent after seven years' separation. Only thirteen years later Parliament introduced divorce by consent after two years' separation and divorce after five years' separation even though the other spouse might object strongly. 'It is obvious that the pressure of hard cases must always tend towards the curtailment of the required period', said the Minority of the Gorell Commission in their separate Report.

There was some disappointment that the Morton Commission was divided on the main issue but its recommendations for changes in the law with regard to such important matters as the position of children, reconciliation, maintenance and collusion were widely welcomed. Amongst critics of the Report, Professor O. R. McGregor was particularly outspoken. Writing in *Divorce in England* he said: 'It is a matter of opinion whether the Morton Commission is intellectually the worst Royal Commission of the twentieth century, but there can be no dispute that its Report is the most unreadable and confused.' In other passages he refers to its Report as 'one of the most impressive collections of unsupported cliché ever subsidised by the tax-payer . . . a soufflé of whipped conjectures'.

He felt that a greater effort should have been made to collect meaningful statistics and that the Commission showed the lack of a trained sociologist amongst its members.

Although the grounds on which a divorce could be obtained remained the same between 1937 and 1969 there were many important changes during this period. As a result of cases decided in the Courts, there were significant alterations in the law relating to cruelty and unsoundness of mind. After the Morton Commission had reported in 1956 there was a considerable volume of change by statute and rule of Court of which the following are some examples:

Maintenance Agreements Act 1957
Matrimonial Causes (Property etc.) Act 1958
Maintenance Orders Act 1958
Divorce (Insanity and Desertion) Act 1958
Mental Health Act 1959
Law Reform (Husband and Wife) Act 1962
Matrimonial Causes Act 1963
Married Women's Property Act 1964
Legal Aid Act 1964
Matrimonial Causes Act 1965
Family Provision Act 1966
Matrimonial Causes Act 1967
Matrimonial Homes Act 1967
Maintenance Orders Act 1968
Domestic and Appellate Proceedings (Restriction of Publicity) Act 1968

There were, in addition, various other Acts more particularly affecting Magistrates' Courts and children and infants. Several of the above Acts put into effect recommendations made by the Morton Commission. However, far more important than any other change and, in my view, the most important Act affecting divorce, apart from the Acts of 1857, 1937 and 1969, was the Legal Aid and Advice Act 1949.

In opposing the Divorce and Matrimonial Causes Bill in the House of Lords on 26 June 1856 the Bishop of Oxford said that 'after giving the best consideration in his power to this subject, he could not doubt that according to the words of our Lord, marriage might be dissolved for the act of adultery; but... it was a matter for further consideration whether it was expedient that Parliament should afford facilities for the dissolution of marriage even for adultery itself'. What worried him was that if divorce was made available in a Court of Law instead of by Act of Parliament how were they going to draw the line between the rich and the poor? '. . . If the facilities to be afforded were not brought down to the lowest class of society, where were they to stop? Were they to reduce the expense of judicial proceedings to such a point that tradesmen might be enabled to obtain divorces, while the opportunity of doing so would be denied to the lower class of the community? Or, were the expenses to be only so far reduced that divorces would be attainable by the richer portion of that middle classes, while they would be beyond the reach of the less wealthy tradespeople? . . . if facilities for divorce were once afforded the gravest dissatisfaction would be produced, unless those facilities were extended to the very lowest classes of society; and . . . such facilities could not be given to the lowest classes without endangering the moral purity of married life.' Furthermore, he was of the opinion that 'the mode which the English Legislature had hit upon—a general prohibition, with the privilege of dissolution in cases which could not be resisted—although a clumsy, and sometimes a very bad mode, was still a much safer and better mode than the introduction of universal laxity, which would follow from the plan proposed'.

In other words, 'I can't say divorce on the grounds of adultery is wrong on religious grounds but if we allow it to be granted in the Courts we shall end up with cheap divorce in the County Court, so let's keep the present system which only a few rich people can afford.' Whatever the merits of this argument it was an accurate forecast of the shape of things to come although the spread to 'the lowest classes' was postponed for a considerable time by the cost of proceedings except in the case of a few very poor people indeed who qualified for assistance under the sketchy system of aid to poor litigants then in force.

According to evidence presented to the Gorell Commission the average minimum cost of an undefended London case was about £40 to £45; if the witnesses had to come from, say, Lancashire the additional cost would be another £12 or £13. By about 1945 the average cost of an undefended divorce was about £70. By 1965 the usual case cost between £90 and £110. If these figures are compared with the fall in the value of the pound it is obvious that divorce has become much cheaper since the end of the nineteenth century and the cost has fallen again since 1965.

Some form of help to enable poor people to bring civil proceedings was started in 1494. In 1883 a new form of procedure was introduced for those worth less than £25. In evidence before the Gorell Commission the following figures were given:

Number of Pauper Petitions filed

Year	By Solicitor	In Person	Total
1907	51	4	55
1908	45	8	53
1909	58	8	66

The total number of decrees nisi granted in the same three years were 598, 672 and 685 respectively. By 1914 the current system had proved so unsatisfactory that new Rules were introduced. These, known as the Poor Persons Rules, lasted until 1950. The applicant for a certificate had to be worth not more than £50 excluding wearing apparel, tools of trade and the subject matter of the intended proceedings and his normal income could not exceed £2 per week.

In exceptional cases his capital position could go up to £100 and his income up to £4 per week. As well as qualifying financially the applicant had to satisfy a panel of solicitors that he had a prima facie case. If certificates were granted, solicitors and counsel were chosen from a rota kept by the Court of those willing to do the work. Eventually the Law Society administered the scheme centrally and local law societies appointed Poor Persons Committees to deal with applications outside London.

The system was inadequate. The financial limits were too low, too many applications were rejected and there was often delay because there were not enough lawyers available. In a series of articles entitled 'Justice Denied' in the *Solicitors' Journal* in 1969 by C. F. Wegg-Prosser the position was summed up as follows:

> 'To no man will we deny, to no man will we sell, or delay, justice or right.'
> This statement in Magna Carta, which was later incorporated into the Constitution of the United States, in itself justifies the case for an effective legal aid system, but it was not until after the second world war that anything like a comprehensive system was established. . . . During the one hundred and fifty years or so that preceded the passing of the Legal Aid and Advice Act 1949, the need for legal advice and representation for the ordinary man became increasingly acute, but the need was most inadequately met. In other words, despite the pledge in Magna Carta, justice was being denied to the citizen.

The Second World War brought the crisis to a head. With vast numbers in the Services, marriages broke down on a rapidly increasing scale and in 1942 the Law Society, working in conjunction with the Service Ministries, set up its Service Divorce Department which, by the middle of 1944, had a staff of sixty and had handled a total of over five and a half thousand cases. In 1944 the Rushcliffe Committee was appointed 'to enquire into the present facilities for giving legal advice and assistance to poor persons' and to make recommendations 'for securing that poor persons have such facilities at their disposal'.

Meanwhile, by the end of the war, over 1,000 Citizens Advice Bureaux had been set up and they had dealt with nine million inquiries.

In 1949 the Legal Aid and Advice Act was passed. The Act and the Rules made under it incorporated many of the features of the previous schemes. There were financial qualifications both as to capital and income and the applicant had to make out a prima facie case to local committees of barristers and solicitors but in future the applicant who was granted a legal aid certificate received the same service from his legal advisers as if he were paying them himself. Unlike the National Health Service legal aid, except for the poorest, was not wholly free. Contributions were demanded based on means, but the applicant knew from the first what his maximum contribution for his own costs would be and it was usually payable by instalments. As it has never been possible for a solicitor to forecast the amount of costs accurately, particularly in divorce cases where it is often not known whether or not the case will be defended or whether or not there will be fights over maintenance, or custody and access, the position of the successful applicant was now very different. Theoretically, if he lost he could be ordered to pay the successful party's costs. In practice, unless there was a substantial improvement in his financial position, he was safe from being ordered to pay anything other than a minor contribution to the other side on top of his assessed maximum contribution.

Apart from contributions by applicants the scheme is financed by the State together with contributions from sums recovered by successful applicants to the extent to which they do not recover costs from the losing party. Lawyers accept a 10% reduction in their High Court fees. Up to 31 March 1968 the State had paid out £46,883,751 in support of the scheme. There had been 659,617 cases brought by legally aided litigants of which 343,243 were matrimonial and 87% of all cases and 91% of matrimonial cases were successful. By 1968 63·3% of matrimonial petitions were filed by legally aided petitioners.

In introducing the Bill into Parliament in 1948, the Attorney-General, Sir Hartley Shawcross, said that it would 'open the doors of the Courts freely to all persons who may wish to avail themselves of British justice without regard to their wealth or ability to pay'. So that if an Egyptian husband domiciled in England files a divorce petition in England his wife living in Egypt will qualify for legal aid in the English Courts and if necessary will receive financial assistance to enable her to come to England for the trial. On the other hand an English wife who has obtained a maintenance order against her former husband cannot get legal aid to enforce the order against him if he goes abroad.

The result of this Act, theoretically, was to open all the Courts, including the Divorce Courts, to everyone. In practice a middle-class husband whose earnings put him outside the scheme, but who could ill afford the costs of a defended case, found himself in an unenviable position. Even before the Act was passed, the fact that he would almost certainly be liable for his wife's costs even if he won, had put him in a weak position. Now the poorer husband could also obtain legal aid and the very rich could afford the cost of litigation. The middle class £1,500 to £2,000 per annum man was left largely defenceless against a wife who pleaded cruelty and obtained legal aid. Even when, belatedly, the financial qualifications have been raised, there has remained a large number of men who are outside the scheme.

Let us now look at a typical defended case fought at the end of the year 1963 with the wife receiving legal aid and the husband on his own. We will assume that the wife is petitioning on the grounds of cruelty and adultery, that the husband is defending the allegation of cruelty, admitting some adultery, but not the adultery pleaded by the wife, and cross-petitioning on the ground of earlier adultery by the wife. The wife's Reply pleads condonation.

When the wife receives a civil aid certificate, a copy must be filed at Court and notice of the fact that she is legally aided given to every other party. No reference to her being legally aided is made in the Petition itself and no reference will be made at the trial until judgment has been pronounced and the Judge is dealing with the question of costs. Nearly always, and particularly in divorce cases, no order is made against a legally aided wife. The husband in this case knows that if he chooses to fight all the way, it is virtually certain that he will have to pay all his own costs even if he wins. If he loses he will probably have to pay her costs as well—the money going to the Legal Aid Fund. There is now an Act (the Legal Aid Act 1964) which allows the Court to order the costs of a non legally aided party to be paid out of the Legal Aid Fund when the other party is legally aided and loses but it has been restrictively interpreted by the Court of Appeal. Recently in a case where the successful non legally aided Defendant had savings of £2,737 and earned about £18 a week gross, an order under this

Act was made in favour of the Defendant. It is unlikely to be applied in favour of a man earning £2,000 a year and upwards. At the time of the case we are now looking at the Act had not even been passed.

Superficially the pleadings would bear a striking resemblance to the pleadings we saw in Chapter 5 and, indeed, most of the details which had to be put in a Petition were still substantially the same.

The most important difference is that as a result of a recommendation of the Morton Commission, the Petitioner's proposals for the care and upbringing of the children have now to be set out when the Petition is filed. This is because the Commission recommended that the law should be changed to provide that a decree nisi should not normally be made absolute unless the Court were satisfied that the arrangements proposed for the care and upbringing of the children were the best which could be devised in the circumstances. This recommendation was given statutory form in the Matrimonial Proceedings (Children) Act 1958 which was re-enacted by the Matrimonial Causes Act 1965, section 33 of which provides as follows:

(1) Notwithstanding anything in Part I of this Act but subject to the following subsection, the court shall not make absolute a decree of divorce or nullity of marriage in any proceedings begun after 31st December 1958, or make a decree of judicial separation in any such proceedings, unless it is satisfied as respects every relevant child who is under sixteen that—
   (a) arrangements for his care and upbringing have been made and are satisfactory or are the best that can be devised in the circumstances; or
   (b) it is impracticable for the party or parties appearing before the court to make any such arrangements.
(2) The court may if it thinks fit proceed without observing the requirements of the foregoing subsection if—
   (a) it appears that there are circumstances making it desirable that the decree should be made absolute or should be made, as the case may be, without delay; and
   (b) the court has obtained a satisfactory undertaking from either or both of the parties to bring the question of the arrangements for the children before the court within a specified time.

Ten years later the Law Commission published a Working Paper containing a report by Mr. John Hall on how this provision had worked out. Mr. Hall put a series of questions to judges, registrars, welfare officers, children's officers and the public and had discussions with some solicitors. He also carried out a small survey based on a random sample of cases chosen from the Cambridge District Registry. The general consensus of opinion seemed to be that section 33 served a useful purpose. The main shortcomings, says Mr. Hall, seem to be that:

> (a) judges are hampered by insufficient time and facilities (and perhaps also by the fact that their experience before appointment was in quite different fields) to enable them at the hearing of the petition to conduct a wholly satisfactory enquiry into the arrangements which are proposed; and in consequence the consideration which they give to the arrangements may often appear to be, and sometimes may actually be, something of a formality;
> (b) apart from the rather formidable sanction of a supervision order there is no machinery to safeguard the child against subsequent disadvantageous changes in the arrangements;
> (c) there is considerable disparity between judges in the use which they make of their existing powers, both to order an enquiry by a welfare officer before approving the arrangements and to order supervision of the child afterwards.

And to quote again:

> There is in fact nothing to stop a petitioner who has obtained a decree nisi on the basis, for example, that she will continue to look after the children, from handing them over to the respondent or to a third person the very next day. A more likely eventuality perhaps, is for the person who has the children to remarry and move to a new home where the conditions in which the children live are quite different from those which obtained at the time of the hearing of the petition.

In practice in the vast majority of undefended cases the position of the children is dealt with in the space of a minute or two, usually on the uncorroborated evidence of the Petitioner alone and there is no subsequent check. Lip-service is paid to the Act and one judge told Mr. Hall that 'this farcical function should be taken away from the judges'. Of those consulted it was mostly the solicitors who considered the present system unsatisfactory. Perhaps they are the people who are most aware of the perfunctory way in which this statutory requirement is complied with in discussion with their clients and in the question or two asked on the hearing of the Petition. At the time of the Morton Commission each year twenty thousand children under the age of sixteen were affected by the divorce of their parents. By 1969 out of a total of approximately twelve million children under the age of sixteen about two million were living in fatherless families and an additional number were living in motherless families. There are fifty Divorce Court welfare officers, of whom four serve in London.

The wife's Petition set out in Chapter 4 refers to 'issue of the said marriage'. The Petition we are now considering would refer to 'children of the family'. The significance of this distinction is summarized in the Preface to the Eighth Edition of *Rayden on Divorce* as follows:

> The legislature in 1958 introduced in a sense a new meaning of 'children', and a new attempt to safeguard their interests at a time when they might otherwise be overlooked. In regard to custody, education and maintenance, the Matrimonial Proceedings (Children) Act, 1958, provides that the idea of 'the family' must prevail; the Court must have regard not merely to the husband and wife and children born of the union of husband and wife, but to the family unit and to all children within that unit. Provided that a child is a child of one party to the marriage and has been accepted into the family, it does not matter what was the ancestry of that child.

The next major change brought about after the Morton Commission's Report was in the law of collusion. After 1963 it became much easier for discussion to take place between the parties and their advisers about maintenance, property and costs. In the case we are now looking at I shall assume that after the exchange of pleadings discussions take place. The wife is alleging that her husband has been cruel. Each alleges that the other has committed adultery. They would like to save the delay, expense and publicity inevitable in a defended cruelty case. Why should not one or other or both get a decree on the ground of adultery subject to their agreeing about the children and financial matters? If they do make such an agreement will the Court allow it to go through?

In January 1965 Mr. Justice Scarman, the Chairman of the Law Commission, tried to give guidance on the new law of collusion when he gave judgment in a group of ten cases (*Nash* v. *Nash*, [1965] P. 266). He began by pointing out that collusion was 'a concept of great range: within it will be found not only such morally offensive bargains as buying false evidence, buying off a defence believed to be good, bribing a reluctant wife to petition by the offer of generous provision after decree absolute, but also such morally inoffensive bargains as the making of reasonable arrangements for maintenance which include a term touching upon the conduct of the suit'. He went on to say that in future 'the general principle is that the Court must be satisfied that it will not, as a result of the agreement, be granting relief for a matrimonial offence which has not occurred or to a party who would not receive relief if the whole of the facts were before the Court. Compendiously put, it is said that the result of the collusive suit must not be contrary to the justice of the case.' He ended by saying:

> . . . a collusive bargain, which represents an honest negotiation between the parties, which is not intended to deceive the Court either by putting forward false evidence or suppressing or withdrawing a good defence and which takes its place in an agreement which is intended to make a reasonable provision for its parties according to its subject matter, is a perfectly reputable transaction. There is no objection to solicitors and counsel negotiating such a bargain: their duty, in this context as in every other, is to apply their honest skill to the task in hand. If they do so and then place the results of their labour before the Court in a spirit of unreserved candour, they will have lived up to the honourable tradition of their profession in a changing world, and will have discharged their duty to their clients, the Court, and the public—the public whose over-riding interest is that the institution of marriage should not be undermined by an unworthy and disreputable market in its dissolution.

In defended cases, therefore, between 1963 and the coming into effect of the Divorce Reform Act 1969 we had the situation where it was possible for a husband and wife to make allegations of cruelty against each other in the Petition and Answer; where they were really fighting only about maintenance; where both subsequently committed adultery and perhaps intended to remarry and where they were both anxious to dispose of the defended cruelty case in which they had become embroiled. Would they be able to bargain their way out of the expensive impasse of the proceedings and get an undefended decree through on, say, the husband's adultery with no maintenance for the wife as she was about to remarry? Answer—yes if it was not contrary to the justice of the case. It then became necessary for counsel to explain to the judge, usually at a preliminary hearing, that although in his Answer the husband had denied his wife's allegations of cruelty and was, on the contrary, saying that she had been cruel to him this was a proper case where there should be no full investigation of the charges and counter-charges of cruelty and that the wife should get a decree on the ground of her husband's adultery. I can only repeat the comment made in the *Solicitors' Journal* in April 1965:

> Under the law of collusion as now defined, the almost incredible position appears to have been reached that, if one party makes insubstantial allegations about the other, a bargain about the conduct of the suit can be made; whereas if the allegations are substantial no bargain can be made. This is a clear inducement to parties to put forward trumped up charges. If under the new procedure Counsel has sought the Court's approval for a proposed arrangement by emphasising the weakness of his client's allegations, what is he to say about those allegations at the trial if the arrangement is not approved at the preliminary hearing?

In practice the change in the law of collusion made a considerable difference in the way divorces were conducted, certainly at least in the case of middle-class wives. Before the change in the law, if the husband wanted a divorce to remarry and the wife was not anxious for a divorce, any attempted bargain by her in which she offered a divorce in return for agreed financial terms was collusive. It was dangerous for the husband to offer any inducement. If, on the other hand, the wife was willing to divorce her husband, but anxious about her financial future and perhaps her security in the matrimonial home, she had to choose either to do nothing or file a Petition. If she did nothing the husband might exert pressure by reducing the maintenance he was paying her or he might force her into Court by himself presenting a Petition based on weak charges of cruelty. Once in Court the wife would usually cross-petition and not merely defend; the husband would then abandon his Petition and tactically would have achieved his purpose.

If the wife herself chose to file a Petition she did so flying completely blind as to what financial provision would be ordered for her at the end of the day. After 1963 all this altered. The parties and their advisers could discuss what financial provision the husband was prepared to make before the wife filed her Petition. Sometimes a bargain was struck quickly; sometimes negotiations were prolonged over months and occasionally years. The terms could be very involved including periodical payments, payment of a capital sum, insurance to cover the loss of pension rights and elaborate provisions to make the payments variable if there were changes in the husband's income to avoid the need and expense of going back to Court for a variation. The question of separate payments for maintenance of the children, income tax and child allowances all had to be considered together with the effect of the Finance Act 1968. The negotiations might well also cover who was to have what furniture with long lists of items claimed and counter-claimed passing to and fro before an agreed list was arrived at. And usually there would be the question of a roof for the wife and children. The agreed provision might vary from an outright gift of a house by the husband to the setting up of a trust to enable the wife to live in the house until the children grew up or until she remarried. It might consist only of an undertaking by the husband to allow his wife to go on residing at the former matrimonial home coupled with his undertaking to continue to pay the mortgage instalments. Since no two couples' financial situation is ever precisely the same, each case involved a re-thinking of the whole problem from the word go.

Finally when agreement was reached it would be put before the Court for its approval. If approved—and approval was not invariable—a decree nisi soon followed. Before 1963 it was only after decree nisi that the fight over maintenance began even in undefended cases.

It will be apparent from what I have written about negotiations over an undefended divorce that it can be quite a complicated affair. One hears of something called easy undefended divorce. Writing in 1953 C. P. Harvey said:

> Large incomes can be made at the Bar out of practices which consist almost entirely of undefended divorces. The hearing of the undefended suit commonly takes between ten and fifteen minutes, though much higher speeds are possible. . . . Counsel are paid at an approximate rate of 12/6d per minute for asking a string of leading questions. The paper work involved in settling documents, advising on evidence, and the like can be done by an experienced practitioner almost in his sleep. . . . It is the fact that undefended divorce works almost on the slot machine principle.

Even he goes on to admit that the work in a defended case is substantial. What he entirely fails to point out is that what goes into the slot machine as an undefended divorce may have looked very different months before. From the solicitor's point of view there are also easy undefended divorces. If he is acting in a case where both parties want a divorce; there are no children; either both wife and husband have means or the wife is remarrying; they have agreed about the furniture and the share each is to have in the proceeds of sale of the matrimonial home; the potential Respondent is already living permanently with someone else; there has been no condonation, connivance or delay; there is no need to ask for the exercise of the Court's discretion—then from the solicitor's point of view it is an easy undefended divorce and I have certainly had a few—a very few. In real life it is all usually rather different and for the vast majority of clients there is no such thing as an easy undefended divorce.

Writing in 1930 H. G. Wells said:

> In regard to divorce, I am probably, by modern standards, sentimental and old fashioned. It seems entirely dreadful to me that two people who have been linked by anything more than a casual encounter, who have gone about as close allies, who have done tender and unselfish things for each other, who have cared for the same things, who have laughed together and made happiness and delight for each other, should be supposed to be capable of a complete mental and physical separation. They must have left a thousand marks upon each other. The severing humiliation, the breach of faith or expectation, the definitive wound or

whatever else it was that has separated them, ought not to efface or corrupt that hoard of memories. Ought not—but I see that it does.

'They must have left a thousand marks upon each other'— they have—and whatever the law of divorce was—even if it were possible to go to a Registry and buy one for £1—there is still for most the anguish of the separation and the problem of sorting out the confused mess into which they are thrown by the separation. No one can make divorce enjoyable because the parting is almost never unalloyed happiness for both. When one has accompanied physically shaking clients through the Victorian Gothic horrors of the Royal Courts of Justice to have their dreams of a happy marriage ended in the nightmare of a shabby room, it makes one angry to hear talk of easy undefended divorce.

It is similar to the talk of colluded divorces—as though in the majority of cases the parties fixed everything up between them in a cosy chat before trotting off to their respective solicitors and hoodwinking them into going on with a faked case. It must happen, but it is not the reality of one's everyday experience when one is as often consulted before the final breakdown as after it by clients desperately anxious for solace and advice and often still doubtfully hoping for a reconciliation or just a little better behaviour from their spouse in the future. When the break is finally recognized as inevitable there are the anxieties over the children and their schools, the home, money, furniture; there are problems over tax, pensions, bank accounts, wills; there is for many the horror of having to discuss the most intimate details of their lives with a stranger, of trying to pin down on paper nuances of cruelty and unkindness which would defeat a leading novelist, of putting into neat chronological order the muddled business of living.

Once it is all in writing and typed out it may look rather different to the barrister who will detect resemblances between one case and another. But every client is different to himself or herself and to the solicitor. By the time the case comes on for hearing in a long undefended list, it has become even more remote from reality to the Judge and for him it will have inevitably taken on something of the atmosphere of the conveyor belt.

In no other branch of civil litigation is the emotional strain on the client and the solicitor greater than in matrimonial disputes. One is dealing with the most important things in life—children, home, the whole financial future. And there is another great difference between divorce work and virtually all other civil litigation. In the latter one is dealing with what is fixed and past—there has been a road accident, someone has been defamed, someone has broken a contract. In matrimonial work one is dealing with the past the present and the future—sometimes at one and the same time. No custody or maintenance order is ever final. What happens where there has been one dispute about access may affect what happens next time—and all the time one tries to remind oneself when one receives another long telephone call of the anguish of the person at the other end of the line.

But let's return for a moment to the case we were looking at. The judge approved of the arrangement for the children set out in the Petition so that the wife got custody and the children went to live with her. The husband visited them at week-ends. After three months she applied for the decree nisi to be made absolute. The husband immediately remarried and for a month or so did not visit the children so often. Then his job took him abroad for a month. On his return home he phoned up his former wife to fix up the next visit to the children. A strange voice answered the phone. He was told that his former wife no longer lived at her old address. No, the speaker did not know her new address but he believed she was in Australia. The husband did not go back to his solicitor. He found out where she had gone, flew to Australia, kidnapped the two children and brought them to his new home.

His former wife was now in a difficult position. She knew that she should not have removed the children out of England without the Court's permission. She had remarried in Australia. She knew when her Petition was heard that she would soon be going to Australia to remarry. She had thought it wise not to tell the judge of her plans at the hearing. What would be the attitude of the English Court if she were now to apply to have the children returned to her? Could she afford the proceedings? Would she have to come to England? She was already pregnant, having had sexual intercourse with her new husband before her second marriage. She hesitated. Her new husband was not very well off. He had accepted her children but now that they had been snatched he did not seem desperately keen to have them back. The days went by in an agony of indecision. Eventually she decided that she must try to get the children back and wrote to her solicitor in England. He explained that she could get legal aid to cover the proceedings (although if she had been in England and the children had been kidnapped to Australia she could not have got legal aid here to bring proceedings there). An application was made to the Court and long affidavits were filed by both sides. What was the Court to do? Whatever the decision the effect would be to bar all access to one parent. Should the children be returned to the mother although she was in the wrong in not having obtained the Court's leave to take them out of the country? Or should they be allowed to stay with their father despite the fact that he had kidnapped them?

Unfortunately in this day of the aeroplane, kidnapping is on the increase. It is so easy to snatch children on their way home from school, bundle them into a car, drive to Heathrow and be at the other side of the world the next day leaving the other parent in the position of having to start proceedings in a strange land often at great expense. The Court does not like kidnapping. In a case in 1968 the Court of Appeal said that the kidnapping tendency had grown far too much in the past few years and it was the duty of every Court not to countenance it. The removal of children by one parent behind the back of the other from the country which was their home was to be condemned unless there was very good reason to the contrary. The children should be returned without more investigation by the Court than was necessary to see that there would be no obvious harm in ordering their return.

On the other hand in a case in 1969 (*Re T* (An Infant) [1969] 1 W.L.R. 1608) where a father, a Swiss national, sought an order that the English mother of their son aged sixteen should return the boy to the father's custody in Switzerland to complete his education in accordance with the terms of a twelve-year-old agreement approved by the Swiss Court the judge took the view that it was essential to know the boy's wishes and said that it was a different case from when younger children were involved and the kidnapping or refusal to return was of recent origin. He said that the boy was neither clearly Swiss nor clearly English but was probably a member of a group of young people 'with international affiliations, connections and qualifications, which was growing as a result of the greater ease of modern travel and international communications'.

In the case we have been looking at, which of the parents removed the children from the country which was their home? Fortunately we do not have to make the decision which faced the judge. The longer the children had been with their father before the Court proceedings were heard the more difficult would the judge's decision have been. He must always do what is in the best interests of the children. In a case of Spanish parents in 1969, this principle was carried by the House of Lords to the extent of excluding both parents from their child and ordering him to remain with a stranger by blood. In that case, which was a wardship case, the proceedings lasted five years. The child had not lived with his parents for seven and a half years. The very length of the proceedings was a powerful factor in influencing the Law Lords to say that the child should remain where he was. Not for the first time in matters concerning custody and care and control of children possession was nine-tenths of the law.

Before we start having a look at the Divorce Reform Act 1969 there are three other important Acts to notice.

For some time there had been anxiety about the effect of the law relating to condonation and collusion on attempts at reconciliation. Usually by the time people whose marriages are breaking up go to see a solicitor it is too late to effect a reconciliation. This is not because solicitors do not want to help in effecting reconciliations. They often do so and are only too delighted if their efforts are successful. The reason is that usually by the time husbands and wives consult their solicitors, attitudes have already hardened completely, but even if there is still the possibility of a reconciliation a visit to a solicitor may be a hindrance rather than a help. Why? Because a solicitor, much as he would like to achieve a reconciliation, is under a duty to his or her client to protect that client's position. That involves discussing the legal rights and wrongs of the situation and a consideration of legal rights and wrongs mixes badly with the give and take, the admission of error and apology and the promise of an attempt to do better, which are the life-blood of a reconciliation. The solicitor has to answer the client's questions but if there is to be a hope of a reconciliation it would often be better that the questions had not been asked.

In some other countries a compulsory reconciliation procedure before a judicial authority has been made a part of the law of divorce. Of these the Denning Committee on Procedure in Matrimonial Causes wrote in February 1947 that 'with the possible exception of the rural cantons of Switzerland these are not a success. In France and Germany they are perfunctory and generally considered as a mere antiquated and superfluous formality. In Holland they have a purely formal character.' This view was confirmed by the Morton Commission who said:

> Most of our witnesses were agreed that various schemes which have been tried in foreign countries, requiring compulsory attendance of parties to a divorce suit before some form of conciliation agency or tribunal, had proved in the end to be a routine and useless formality.

The Morton Commission accepted the views of those engaged in marriage counselling that 'it would be unwise to attempt to define any formal pattern of conciliation agencies, or to set up an official conciliation service. The State's role should rather be to give every encouragement to the existing agencies, statutory and voluntary, engaged in matrimonial conciliation. . . .'

The Commission recommended the continuation of Exchequer Grants towards the work, grants which were ludicrously small compared with the cost of divorce.

As to collusion and condonation the Commission said that the law 'should be such that it will not act as a deterrent to bringing husband and wife together with a view to reconciliation. Where one of them has ground for divorce he may often fear that any meeting or discussion with the other may endanger his case and thus may be hesitant to make or respond to any approach. And if he agrees to enter wholeheartedly into an attempt at reconciliation he may run the risk, if the attempt should subsequently prove unsuccessful, of being held to have condoned the other spouse's offence. Such fears and doubts may in particular arise to prevent husband and wife coming together where one of them is in desertion.'

Mr. Leo Abse, an M.P. and a practising solicitor, with the active support of the Law Society, took the hint and the result was the Matrimonial Causes Act of 1963 which amended the law of collusion and also contained the 'kiss and make up' provisions as follows:

1. Any presumption of condonation which arises from the continuance or resumption of marital intercourse may be rebutted on the part of a husband, as well as on the part of a wife, by evidence sufficient to negative the necessary intent.

2. (1) For the purposes of the Matrimonial Causes Act 1950, and of the Matrimonial Proceedings (Magistrates' Courts) Act 1960, adultery or cruelty shall not be deemed to have been condoned by reason only of a continuation or resumption of cohabitation between the parties for one period not exceeding three months, or of anything done during such cohabitation, if it is proved that cohabitation was continued or resumed, as the case may be, with a view to effecting a reconciliation.

(2) In calculating . . . the period for which the respondent has deserted the petitioner without cause, and in considering whether such desertion has been continuous, no account shall be taken of any one period (not exceeding three months) during which the parties resumed cohabitation with a view to a reconciliation.

3. Adultery which has been condoned shall not be capable of being revived.

In the nature of things there can be no statistical evidence on how effective these provisions have been in helping reconciliations. Unfortunately if a solicitor is consulted say by a wife before she returns for a trial period to a husband who has been committing adultery, he is bound to point out that there are snags in the section. The wife may return genuinely hoping for a reconciliation and so may the husband. But what happens if, after two months, the wife feels that the attempt at a reconciliation has been a failure while the husband says that there has been a reconciliation. In other words the Act protects a couple when they both want a trial period to attempt a reconciliation and both agree that things have not worked out. But if only one says it has been a failure, the other can still argue that, as in this example, his adultery has been condoned—and now condoned for all time—so that the wife will have to wait for fresh evidence of adultery before she can seek her freedom.

Condonation of a matrimonial offence was defined in a case in 1969 as the reinstatement in his or her former matrimonial position of a spouse who has committed a matrimonial wrong of which all material facts are known to the other spouse with the intention of forgiving and remitting the wrong. Forgiveness meant an intention, express or to be implied, to remit a right to complain of a matrimonial injury and reinstatement might be inferred merely from a resumption or continuance of cohabitation. Affection, it was held, was not a necessary element in either forgiveness or reinstatement. The facts in that case were a long way from the three months' trial period but difficulties have arisen in several other cases on the 'kiss and make up' provisions.

In the late sixties the financial position of wives was still improving. It was at last beginning to be realized that a wife might be entitled to more by way of maintenance than under the old so-called 'one-third rule'. For middle-class wives the change in the law of collusion meant that she could often bargain for a fairer provision for herself and the children and in respect of the furniture and home. The law had been strengthened to prevent dispositions of property by husbands to defeat their wives' claims; the Court was given power to order a husband to make a capital payment to his wife, though the power was sparingly used; husbands who chose to live on capital and who had no income for income tax purposes found that the Court would look at the reality of the situation and make an order against them.

Divorced wives were given the right to apply to the Court for provision out of their deceased former husband's estate. Wives were given the right to retain as their own property half the savings they made from their housekeeping allowance. Even wives who were guilty of a matrimonial offence could expect more generous treatment.

It still remained true, however, that when a wife was seeking adequate financial provision from a wily, obstinate, and wealthy husband, she could often be put to endless trouble in obtaining a fair order or in later enforcing it. She might therefore be well advised to accept less than the amount to which she was strictly entitled in order to get regular payments. And in one area of law—perhaps the most important—namely that of the matrimonial home the law was in a complete mess. Ever since the Second World War there has been a flood of cases relating to the wife's right to the matrimonial home. The mess has arisen out of the attempt by the Courts to create for the wife rights which could only with difficulty be fitted into the previous law of property. Some judges tried to stretch the law to help the deserted or divorced wife and her children. Others thought that the old law could not be enlarged to deal with the situation of the divorced wife and husband where the precise circumstances were never the same. Sometimes the house was solely in the husband's name; sometimes in the names of both husband and wife. Sometimes both had contributed to the initial deposit; sometimes one had done so; sometimes the parents of one or other had contributed. The wife might or might not have worked. If she had worked she might or might not have contributed to the mortgage repayments, directly or indirectly. Since the house had been bought the value would almost certainly have increased—how was the increase in value to be shared on the break-up of the marriage? Improvements might have been made from the installation of central heating or the addition of a room down to 'do it yourself' running repairs. And was the conduct of the parties in causing the break-up of the marriage to be taken into account?

For five days in February 1969 a case was argued in the House of Lords in which the law of the matrimonial home was considered (*Pettitt* v. *Pettitt*, [1969] 2 W.L.R. 966). Some sixty cases in the Law Reports were referred to of which thirty-nine were cases decided after the Second World War. The case was about a husband's claim to share in the proceeds of the matrimonial home based on his having done work on the house by way of redecoration and improvement which he said had enhanced its value by £1,000. The Registrar and the Court of Appeal held that he was entitled to share in the proceeds to the extent of £300. The House of Lords overruled the decision of the Court of Appeal.

Since that case was decided there have already been several other cases which have reached the Court of Appeal. For years it has been a matter of great difficulty to advise a client with assurance about the respective rights of the spouses in the matrimonial home. If an agreement could not be negotiated and the case were fought all the way the result might turn on the composition of the Court of Appeal when the appeal was heard.

In the course of his judgment in the case referred to above, Lord Reid said:

> We were informed that last year there were nine hundred applications in the High Court besides an unknown number in the County Courts. The whole question can only be resolved by Parliament and in my opinion there is urgent need for comprehensive legislation.

The same view had been expressed by a much less erudite lawyer and in slightly more forceful language in an article in the *Solicitors' Journal* four years earlier when he said:

> From the law of real property, equity, the Married Women's Property Act, 1882, and palm tree justice, an inglorious and uncertain shambles has been produced which is a disgrace to the profession and can only be remedied by legislation.

One attempt at legislation has been made—the Matrimonial Homes Act 1967. Thanks to the efforts of Lady Summerskill—that pugnacious opponent of pugilism who defends women's rights with masculine vigour—an Act was passed to give some degree of protection to the wife. In 1965 a House of Lords decision had weakened the position of the deserted wife. The Act, in effect, distinguishes between rights of ownership and rights of occupation. It gives the spouse who is not the owner or tenant a right, if in occupation, not to be evicted without an order of the Court, and, if not in occupation, a right, with the leave of the Court, to enter and occupy the dwelling. By registration the rights of occupation can be protected not only against a spouse but also against any purchaser, mortgagee or donee whose interest arises subsequent to the registration.

This is an important Act for the protection of wives (and also of husbands) but it does not touch the more complex questions referred to by Lord Reid and which are now being studied by the Law Commission.

In making his Minority Report to the 1853 Royal Commission Report Lord Redesdale wrote:

My apprehensions of evil consequences, however, extend still further. I consider the tribunal recommended by the Commissioners for determining these questions a very good one; but proceedings before it in cases of Divorce ā vinculo will necessarily be attended with some expense, though far below that which is now required. These Divorces will thus be opened to another and numerous class, but a still more numerous class will be equally excluded as at present. Once create an appetite for such licence by the proposed change, and the demand to be permitted to satisfy it will become irresistible. The cry for cheap law has of late been universally attended to, and the result will too probably be that these delicate and important questions will be brought before inferior tribunals, where the number of the judges (each acting separately) will render anything like uniformity of decision upon the circumstances which are to rule in refusing applications, impossible, and must ultimately lead to extreme facility in obtaining such Divorces.

For these reasons I am unable to concur in the Report agreed upon by the other Commissioners in all that relates to Divorce ā vinculo, as in my opinion it is expedient—

That the law of England, which now holds the marriage tie to be indissoluble, should remain unaltered; and

That the practice of passing exceptional laws in favour of particular cases should henceforth be discontinued.

I concur in the other recommendations of the Report.

The Bishop of St Davids in the subsequent debate also foresaw the same consequences.

The Gorell Commission received a good deal of evidence on the hardship inflicted because divorce work was confined to the High Court in London. The Majority made the following recommendations:

I.—UNDER PART X.

(1) That the High Court should hold sittings and exercise jurisdiction locally for the purpose of hearing and determining divorce and other matrimonial causes by Commissioners appointed for that purpose.

(2) That the country should be apportioned into districts corresponding with the present circuits of the High Court, subject to such modifications as might prove convenient, and a metropolitan district.

(3) That there should be a Commissioner for each district or combination of districts who should be selected by the Lord Chancellor from among the county court judges or persons qualified to be appointed Commissioners of Assize, with power, if it were found necessary or convenient to have more than one Commissioner for a district, to add another.

(4) That the Commissioner, while in office as such, should have all the powers of a judge of the High Court of Justice and all the jurisdiction of the High Court of Justice in these cases, subject to rules of practice as stated.

(5) That the sittings should be at each place where there is a registry of the High Court, and at such other place or places at which the Lord Chancellor should think sittings may be reasonably required, and that registries should be established at such place or places with the necessary powers.

II.—UNDER PART XI.

(1) That the actual exercise of jurisdiction locally should in practice be confined to cases in which the joint income of the petitioner and the respondent is not more than £300 per annum and the assets not more than £250.

(2) That simplified procedure and practice for these cases as explained in detail should be adopted, special tables of fees and costs fixed, and provisions (as suggested in Part XVI.) made as to proceedings in formâ pauperis.

In a Note to the Majority Report His Honour Judge Tindal Atkinson said:

> I fully concur in the suggestion contained in this Report that the court appointed to try divorce cases should be the High Court, in courts presided over by certain county court judges put into commission for such purpose, or, if necessary, other Commissioners travelling through appointed circuits for the trial of matrimonial causes.
>
> I believe that procedure will give the necessary facilities to enable the poorer classes to obtain relief provided the Commissioners hold their sittings in a sufficient number of towns so that the courts are really accessible to and available for these classes in all parts of the country.

In agreeing to this suggestion I am materially influenced by the consideration that it effectually meets the objection made by a considerable number of persons, many of them very influential, who, rightly regarding the marriage contract as being of the most solemn character not only affecting the parties to it but the welfare of the State, are of opinion that questions affecting the dissolution of marriage should be tried and decided in the Supreme Court.

I desire, however, to record my opinion that should the Legislature at any time decide to confer upon the county courts this jurisdiction it will be exercised and justice administered with complete satisfaction.

Nothing was done about the recommendation that selected County Court judges should be appointed to sit as Commissioners of the High Court, although cases were tried on Assize and District Registries set up.

In October 1946 the Denning Committee on Procedure in Matrimonial Causes made its Second Interim Report. The Courts were swamped with the immediate post-war flood of divorce. On this question they said:

The question of Courts has already received much consideration by Royal Commissions and by Committees. We have had further evidence upon it and have further considered it, and we desire specifically to re-affirm the principle stated by the Royal Commission of 1912 that 'the gravity of divorce and other matrimonial cases affecting as they do the family life, the status of the parties, the interests of their children, and the interests of the State in the moral and social well-being of its citizens, makes it desirable to provide, if possible, that, even for the poorest persons, these cases should be determined by the Superior Courts of the country, assisted by the attendance of the Bar, which we regard as of high importance in divorce and matrimonial cases, both in the interest of the parties and in the public interest'. In our opinion the attitude of the community towards the status of marriage is much influenced by the way in which divorce is effected. If there is a careful and dignified proceeding such as obtains in the High Court for the undoing of a marriage, then quite unconsciously the people will have a much more respectful view of the marriage tie and of the marriage status than they would if divorce were effected informally in an inferior court.

They recommended that the High Court jurisdiction should

be maintained in London and the provinces, but that undefended divorce cases should no longer be tried by High Court
judges as part of the ordinary work of Assizes. They also suggested that County Court judges should be appointed Commissioners for matrimonial causes to supplement the number of
High Court judges. They made a number of proposals to cut
out unnecessary steps in divorce procedure. A large number of
their proposals were acted on including the suggestion about
County Court judges. Speaking in the House of Lords on
14 February 1967 Lord Gardiner described this as 'The usual
brilliant English compromise; namely that undefended cases—
and, indeed some defended ones—should be heard by County
Court judges dressed up as High Court judges for the day.'

The Morton Commission, describing the results of the compromise, said that the system had the merit of being very
flexible and seemed on the whole to have worked well. They
said, however, that they had received some evidence 'suggesting that the highest standards of presentation and trial have not
always been attained in individual cases'. They went on to say
that they regarded it as most important that very great care
should be taken over undefended cases. 'They may be neither
easy nor straightforward and some pains may be necessary to
get at the truth. But, whatever trouble may be required, it is
essential that people should realise that divorce is a serious
matter, and that it does not follow that a decree is always
granted if the case is undefended.' They hoped that there would
be a return 'as soon as possible to the system under which all
cases, defended and undefended, are tried by judges of the
High Court'.

They hoped in vain. In 1966 County Court judges tried
34,000 out of a total of 38,000 undefended cases. They also
tried 894 of the shorter defended cases.

In 1967 the Matrimonial Causes Act of that year transferred the hearing of undefended divorce to the County Courts.
We have moved a long way since the Act of 1857 provided
expressly that the judges to hear matrimonial suits should be
limited to the Lord Chancellor, the Chief Justices of the three
Common Law Courts and four other senior High Court judges.
County Court Registrars whose jurisdiction in other matters is
limited to a trifling amount will have unlimited jurisdiction in

financial matters connected with undefended divorce petitions even though the financial matters are themselves the subject of a bitter fight. Presumably Lord Redesdale and the Bishop of St. Davids turned in their graves.

Whether Parliament fully realized that it was also transferring fights about custody and maintenance to the County Court provided the Petition itself was undefended is not clear.

At this time, before the Divorce Reform Act 1969, the position of the wife was stronger than it had ever been. Although, except in the case of the very wealthiest, the standard of living of both wife and husband is bound to go down after a divorce she had achieved complete equality so far as the grounds for divorce were concerned; in practice her rights in respect of the children were stronger than the husband's; financially the tide was still moving in her favour; if she had resided in England or Wales for three years, she could always petition, whereas her husband could not file a petition for divorce based on residence alone; so far as the cost of proceedings was concerned Legal Aid helped her and sometimes put her in a stronger position than her husband. Perhaps her position was never to be as strong again.

7

THE END OF MARRIAGE—1970 ONWARDS

*In Sweden, one of the most highly civilised countries in the world,
a marriage is dissolved if both parties wish it without any question of
conduct. That is what marriage means in Sweden. In Clapham that is
what they call by the senseless name of Free Love. . . . The husband,
then, is to be allowed to discard his wife when he is tired of her, and
the wife the husband when another man strikes her fancy? One must
reply unhesitatingly in the affirmative. . . .*

GEORGE BERNARD SHAW: From the Preface to *Getting Married*
(1908)

*There is no pressing necessity for dealing with the question at the
moment . . . there are no petitions or anxiety on the part of the public.*

W. E. GLADSTONE: House of Commons, 24 July 1857

*I cannot help feeling that more noise has been made, both in Parlia-
ment and in certain sections of the Press, with regard to this Bill than
is warranted by public opinion outside. I know well enough that too much
importance must not be attached to what happens on a Friday in another
place. The fact remains that out of 600 Members of Parliament in
the other place only 227 turned up to vote one way or the other on the
Third Reading of the Bill. That does not point to any great extent of
violent enthusiasm on behalf of the measure.*

VISCOUNT FITZALAN OF DERWENT: House of Lords, 24 June 1937

*Quite understandably, a tremendous amount of information was dis-
seminated in another place by the promoters of the Bill, yet after all that
propaganda only one quarter of the Members—totalling six hundred—of
another place voted for or against this Bill. This cannot be regarded as
representing the will of the British people on divorce, and certainly not
the will of the inarticulate women and children who may be the victims
of this Bill.*

BARONESS SUMMERSKILL: House of Lords, 30 June 1969

*I assume, and I think I am entitled to do so, that there will be many
to-day who will stay away not because they are really against the Bill*

or because they are really for it, but because they feel that it might do them some personal harm in their constituency. I have no quarrel with those who, on conscientious or religious grounds, oppose the Bill, but I do quarrel very much with those who through apathy or, worse still, through cowardice, stay away.

MR. DE LA BERE: House of Commons, 20 November 1936

Lord Stow Hill: [This Bill] does not undermine the institution of divorce: it does precisely the opposite. . . .

Viscount Dilhorne: The noble Lord said that it does not undermine the institution of divorce. I think he must have meant the institution of marriage.

Lord Stow Hill: My Lords, I was so carried away by my enthusiasm that my logic, I am afraid, gave way to my impulse.

House of Lords, 13 October 1969

In the years immediately following the Morton Commission's Report the annual number of decrees absolute remained at about twenty-two or twenty-three thousand. In his book *Britain in the Sixties—The Family and Marriage* published in 1962 Ronald Fletcher wrote:

Frequently . . . it is said that divorce has been continually increasing during the past few decades. This statement is simply not true. If we take roughly the past fifty years, the incidence of divorce begins to increase sharply just before and continues to increase until just after 1918; then it declines (but not to the pre-war level) and remains fairly steady until just before 1939. It increases again during the war years until shortly after 1945 (the peak being in 1947). Then there follows another decline until about 1950 when legal aid for divorce was effectively introduced. Here the incidence of divorce remains steady for a time and then gradually decreases until the present day. Although there is a large quantity of divorce, therefore, it is quite wrong to say that divorce is continually increasing. . . . With the return of settled peace-time conditions, divorce seems always to have a tendency to decrease.

L

During the sixties the annual number of Decrees Absolute was as follows:

1960	23,369
1961	24,936
1962	28,376
1963	31,405
1964	34,162
1965	37,084
1966	38,352
1967	42,378
1968	45,036

Speaking in the House of Lords on 30 June 1969 Lord Stow Hill (the former Labour Solicitor-General Sir Frank Soskice) prophesied that if the Divorce Reform Bill were passed, it might result after 'an initial backlog' in an extra 5,000 divorces a year in this country, 'with a consequent increase in the cost of the Legal Aid Scheme, equal to a small fraction of the cost of building the *Queen Elizabeth*—cheap at the price for the relief of the massive suffering involved'.

Parliament's response to these statistics, actual and prophesied, was to pass the Divorce Reform Act 1969, thereby introducing divorce by consent after two years' separation and divorce against the will of a spouse after five years' separation. Speaking in the debate on the 1857 Act, Sir William Heathcote said: 'The only consistent conclusion of such a course of legislation was to declare that even the mutual consent of the parties was sufficient to dissolve a marriage.' After a fight lasting nearly 2,000 years, the Church had been defeated. Subject to the separation having lasted five years we are back to the position in Roman law in the late Republic and early Empire thus described by Lecky:

> Being looked upon merely as a civil contract, entered into for the happiness of the contracting parties, its continuance depended upon mutual consent. Either party might dissolve it at will, and the dissolution gave both parties a right to remarry. There can be no question that under this system the obligations of marriage were treated with extreme levity. . . . Seneca denounced this evil with especial vehemence, declaring that divorce in Rome no longer brought with it any shame, and that there were women

who reckoned their years rather by their husbands than by the consuls. . . . According to Tertullian 'divorce is the fruit of marriage'. Martial speaks of a woman who had already arrived at her tenth husband; Juvenal, of a woman having eight husbands in five years . . .

Writing in 1953 of the significance of modern marriage and, echoing Tertullian, C. P. Harvey, Q.C., said

> . . . the point is that you must have a valid marriage before you can have a divorce. Indeed it is the only condition precedent to divorce which cannot be circumvented somehow.

Although they were slow starting, things have moved fast over the last thirty years, but even before that, as we have seen, divorce by consent against the will of one party had its advocates in evidence before the Gorell Commission. Shaw was advocating complete freedom to get out of marriage in 1908. The Gorell Commission itself in its Majority Report wrote of mutual consent:

> Some persons consider this as the only solution of the difficulties of married life under the conditions of modern civilisation; and divorce at the will of one party, subject to suitable restrictions, has even been advocated by others. These suggestions have met with little support from any of the numerous witnesses who have been called before us, and are not likely to meet with any substantial support at the present day in England. . . . Accordingly, we do not recommend these two causes (i.e. mutual consent and incompatibility of temper) as grounds of divorce.

On this the Minority of the Gorell Commission commented in their Report:

> In other words, divorce for incompatibility and divorce by mutual consent are laid aside, not because they violate any principle on which the Majority Report is based, but merely because, for the moment, no effective demand for them can be discerned. But the inevitable conclusion of the premises adopted by our colleagues cannot be evaded. The evidence of several witnesses of distinction in different ways shows that they, at any rate, accept the position.

Not only was the Gorell Commission prepared to contemplate (although not recommend) without horror divorce by mutual consent—the Majority actually did recommend divorce against the will of a spouse. Paragraph 392 (the italics are mine) of the Majority Report reads: 'We recommend that the Court should have power, in its discretion, when a decree of separation is asked for on grounds found by the Court which would justify a decree of divorce, to make a decree of divorce *on the application of the respondent.*' Mr. J. A. Spender would have gone even further; he was in favour of giving such respondents 'the *right,* on application to the Court, of having a decree of separation converted into a decree of divorce after the lapse of two years'. This was too much for Mrs. May Tennant, the first woman to be appointed a factory inspector, who wrote: 'I cannot feel that the guilty person should have any power to impose upon the innocent a remedy against which he or she may have conscientious scruples.' The Minority merely recorded their disagreement on this point.

In February 1947 the Denning Committee in their First Report said:

> In the course of our examination of the administration of the law, we have received many suggestions for reforms in the substantive law as to the grounds of divorce. It is outside our terms of reference to make recommendations on these matters, but it may be useful if we set down the principal suggestions for consideration. . . .
>
> (iii) There appears to be a large number of cases where husband and wife have been separated for many years and there is no possibility of their ever coming together again, but a divorce cannot be obtained because the separation was by mutual consent and did not amount in law to desertion. It is suggested for consideration whether separation for seven years or more should not be a ground of divorce if there is no prospect of reconciliation.

In 1950 Mrs. Eirene White introduced in the House of Commons a Bill of which, in her own words, 'the main purpose . . . was to secure accceptance of the principle that the de facto breakdown of a marriage to an extent which ruled out reasonable hope of reconciliation, should in itself be considered a ground for legal dissolution'. The House of Commons gave the Bill a Second Reading but the Bill was withdrawn in Committee because the Government undertook to appoint a Royal Commission which later became known as the Morton Commission.

In the same year in a case in the Court of Appeal Lord Justice Denning, as he then was, said:

> The Court is not at liberty to grant divorces simply because the marriage has utterly broken down. It might be a good thing if it could do so after long years of separation even if the separation was originally by agreement or for some cause short of cruelty.

In 1951 in *The Reform of the Law* the Society of Labour Lawyers recommended divorce by consent and divorce for separation against the will of a spouse. As to the former, safeguards were suggested to ensure the consent was genuine and that all hope of a reconciliation had failed. It was suggested that the proposal would avoid the squalor, collusion and perjury found in the Divorce Court. As to divorce after separation they wrote:

> It often happens that, although one spouse has committed a matrimonial offence and it is obvious to all concerned that cohabitation will not be resumed, the other spouse refuses to file a petition. The motives for such refusal vary from religious conviction, through forlorn hope to sheer spite; the result is the same— a marriage is nominally kept on the register without any basis in fact.
>
> It is in the public interest that such dead marriages should be decently buried. Both parties might then, if they wished, live in new marriages instead of being compelled to live either in celibacy or in sin, and they would both be brought to face the future instead of remaining buried in the past, and might forget an unfortunate episode in their lives instead of being continually reminded of it.
>
> In these circumstances, where the fact that a marriage has broken down is shown by the fact that, for whatever reason, the parties have been separated for over two years, either party should be entitled to a divorce at the discretion of the Court, and after separation for three years the divorce should be as of right.

In 1953 New Zealand allowed divorce when the parties were living apart, unlikely to be reconciled and had been living apart for not less than seven years, but the Court was bound to refuse a decree if the separation was due to the wrongful act or conduct of the Petitioner.

In 1956 the Morton Commission reported and, as we have seen, was split on the principle of breakdown. In 1961 Australia allowed divorce for wilful desertion for two years and also where the parties had separated and thereafter lived separately and apart for a continuous period of not less than five years immediately preceding the date of the Petition and there was no reasonable likelihood of cohabitation being resumed. The Court was bound to refuse a decree on the latter ground when to do so would be 'harsh and oppressive to the Respondent or contrary to the public interest'.

In 1963 Mr. Leo Abse introduced a Bill which contained in addition to the 'kiss and make up' provisions other proposals similar to those in Mrs. Eirene White's Bill. The Bill became the Matrimonial Causes Act 1963 but the controversial clauses were dropped in order to ensure the passing of the 'kiss and make up' provisions.

In 1963 *Law Reform Now* was published, edited by Gerald Gardiner, Q.C., later Lord Chancellor, and Mr. Andrew Martin, later a member of the Law Commission whose setting up the book recommended. In the chapter on Family Law there is the following passage (the italics are mine):

> We believe that the provisions of the new Family Charter should clearly reflect those general principles of family life on which our modern society is based. At the risk of restating *what to most must be obvious*, we would summarise those principles as follows:—
>
> (1) Men and women are equal before the law.
> (2) Marriage is neither an insurance policy for women, designed to keep them in economic security, nor is it a conveyance of property.
> (3) Marriage imposes rights and duties on both spouses; marriages break down because one spouse is (more usually both are) in breach of some of those duties.
> (4) So far as the law is concerned, marriage is dissoluble. Parties to a marriage which has completely broken should never find themselves irretrievably tied to each other.
> (5) Children are entitled to a special protection and are not to be treated as pawns in a battle between their parents.

They went on to recommend that 'when spouses have lived apart for five years, either party should be entitled to present a petition—the length of the separation being sufficient evidence of the breakdown'.

On 21 June 1963 in the course of a debate on Mr. Abse's Bill the Archbishop of Canterbury, Dr. Ramsey, said:

> If it were possible to find a principle at law of breakdown of marriage which was free from any trace of the idea of consent, which conserved the point that offences and not only wishes, are the basis of the breakdown, and which was protected by a far more thorough insistence on reconciliation procedure first, then I would wish to consider it. Indeed, I am asking some of my fellow churchmen to see whether it is possible to work at this idea, sociologically as well as doctrinally, to discover if anything can be produced.

In January 1964 he appointed a Committee which reported in *Putting Asunder* in July 1966 strongly in favour of introducing the principle of breakdown. They said that:

> ... choosing between the doctrine of the matrimonial offence and the doctrine of breakdown of marriage remains, when all has been said, a choice of evils ... our claim, therefore, is the modest one, that of the alternatives available to contemporary society, a law based on breakdown would be the lesser evil by a very considerable way.

The Committee emphasized that in their view the principle of breakdown must not be introduced into a law based on the matrimonial offence because 'the mutual incompatibility of the two principles would be glaringly obvious ... the superficiality inseparable from verbally formulated "grounds" would tend to render the principle of breakdown inoperative... the addition of a new "ground" embodying the principle of breakdown would make divorce easier to get without really improving the law'. They also recommended that there should be an absolute bar on divorce where to grant a divorce would be 'contrary to the public interest in justice. ... This provision would do something to discourage the unscrupulous from thinking that desertion and the formation of an irregular union would in due course win a decree automatically.'

The next thing that happened was that in November 1966 the Law Commission reported to the Lord Chancellor, Lord Gardiner, giving its views on *Putting Asunder* in *Reform of the Grounds of Divorce—The Field of Choice*. The Law Commission rejected the recommendation of the Archbishop's Committee as 'procedurally impracticable'. The thorough inquest into the marriage in every divorce case which the Archbishop's Committee proposed would not be 'feasible, even if it were desirable . . . because of the time this would take and the costs involved'. In the words of George Farquhar in *The Beaux Stratagem* in 1707: 'Can a jury sum up the endless aversions that are rooted in our souls, or can a bench give judgment upon antipathies?'

Back to square one? No—there were meetings between members of the Archbishop's Committee and the Law Commission and on 2 June 1967 the Law Commission reported on these talks. In place of the inquest proposed in *Putting Asunder* the Court was to be directed to infer breakdown, in the absence of evidence to the contrary, 'on proof of the existence of certain matrimonial situations'. Proposals were then set out, Number 5 of which was as follows:

(1) No marriage should be treated as having broken down irretrievably unless the Court was satisfied that:—
    (a) the respondent had committed adultery and the petitioner found it intolerable to continue or resume cohabitation; or
    (b) the conduct of the respondent had been so intolerable that the petitioner could not reasonably be expected to continue or resume cohabitation; or
    (c) the parties had ceased to cohabit for a continuous period of at least two years and the respondent either
        (i) had deserted the petitioner, or
        (ii) did not object to the grant of a divorce; or
    (d) the parties had ceased to cohabit for a continuous period of not less than five years.
(2) If the Court was satisfied that any of the above situations existed, it should treat the marriage as having broken down irretrievably unless satisfied on all the evidence that the marriage had not broken down irretrievably.

On 29 November 1967 Mr. Wilson introduced a Bill giving effect to the above proposals. It failed to get through Parliament because of lack of time and was reintroduced by Mr. Alec Jones in November 1968. The Divorce Reform Act received the Royal Assent on 22 October 1969, coming into effect on 1 January 1971.

It did not contain the absolute bar advocated by the Archbishop's Committee to prevent glaring injustice. Under a thin disguise it preserved the doctrine of matrimonial offence which that Committee declared to be incompatible with the principle of breakdown. It was another typically English and completely illogical compromise.

Amongst the many voices which were heard during the Parliamentary debates on the 1967 and 1968 Bills that of the President of the Probate Divorce and Admiralty Division, Sir Jocelyn Simon, was not included. Unlike the Lord Chancellor, the Lord Chief Justice, and the Master of the Rolls, he had no seat in the Lords. What he had said some years before in a speech to the Law Society's Annual Conference in 1965 was ignored. The speech was called *The Seven Pillars of Divorce Reform*, and the seven pillars were: justice; human kind's division of labour; the institution of marriage; the children's welfare; finance; realism; relief. He said:

> The central pillar must be the pillar of justice. From this spring arches to all the others; and however intricate the final vaulting, we must be able to trace the structural lines back to the pillar of justice. The pillar of justice establishes that the law should not assist anyone to gain an advantage from his own wrong doing, particularly if it causes injury to an innocent party.

Whether or not the pillar of justice is strengthened by the new Act it is now the law and I propose to consider what is likely to happen as a result of its provisions which started to affect advice to clients long before it came into effect. Speaking in the House of Lords on 13 October 1969 Lord Reid said that:

> ... ninety-five per cent of the cases which come before the divorce court will go on in exactly the same way and have exactly the same result as if this bill had never been passed.

I am not sure that the figure will be as high as 95% but it is likely that there will still be a very large number of Petitions based on adultery and on the new version of cruelty which does not need medical evidence in its support. There may well be, at first, a flood of five-year cases and a considerable number of divorces by consent. In introducing the Divorce Reform Bill on the Second Reading in the House of Lords on 30 June 1969, speaking of divorce by consent Lord Stow Hill said:

Your Lordships may hope that if divorce on this ground is allowed this is the method which more and more will be used by well-behaved people, and the sordid recitals of adulterous behaviour which now degrade our courts will be increasingly consigned to the dustbin where they belong.

I disagree with this prophecy and I shall try to explain why.

It is true that under the law as it existed before the Divorce Reform Act 1969 if the parties separated by consent and no matrimonial offence had been committed there could be no divorce. Such people will now be able to obtain a divorce by consent under the new Act after two years' separation—if they can agree on financial terms. If not, they will have to wait another three years so that one side can then petition on the five years' ground or one of them will have to commit adultery as now.

If in future a husband and wife cannot get on together and decide that they must go in for a divorce but that they do not wish to throw mud at each other, they may well wish to use the provision for divorce by consent. So perhaps they will, as some already have done, go to their solicitor and ask how they set about it. The solicitor will have to point out that if the parties have not yet separated and they are about to separate, then, although they may agree in principle with the idea of divorce by consent, it may not be certain that they will be in agreement in two years' time about the financial provisions which are to be made. If not, there will not be any divorce by consent and no divorce on desertion because the initial parting has been by agreement.

Moreover, although there may be a backlog of cases where the parties have been apart for two years or part of two years by agreement and can agree financial terms so that they can get a divorce by consent by 1972, I believe that we shall find, as now, that in effect most marriages have broken up because the husband or wife has gone off either with or without someone else and at least one of them does not want to wait two years for a divorce by consent. He or she will want it sooner and may well go on the old grounds of adultery or cruelty. If the wife has been left by her husband who has gone off with another woman and the husband wants a divorce but the wife either does not or is not in a hurry for one the husband will seek to persuade his wife to divorce him on the ground of adultery. If the wife eventually agrees, being satisfied with the husband's financial proposals, she will petition on adultery and get an agreed financial order. It will be in one sense a divorce by consent as it was under the law before the Divorce Reform Act 1969, but it will not be divorce by consent after two years' separation.

Even if the wife and husband do not agree on financial terms, they may both want a divorce quickly, in which case in the circumstances I have just outlined, the wife might petition on adultery and leave financial matters to be decided by the Court. If so a case in the Court of Appeal on 2 December 1969 will help them (*Tumath* v. *Tumath*, [1970] 2 W.L.R. 169). In that case a wife petitioned for divorce on the ground of her husband's adultery, admitting that she herself had committed adultery. The husband did not defend his wife's Petition, but when the question of maintenance came up after the decree nisi he wanted to allege that he should not pay as much maintenance as he might otherwise have been ordered to pay because his wife had deserted him before he committed adultery. The County Court judge following previous High Court decisions said he could not do so. The Court of Appeal said he could; Lord Justice Salmon said that—

> On the public policy ground, it was well settled that in exercising discretion in proceedings for permanent maintenance it was of the utmost importance for the Court to have regard to the conduct of the parties: *Restall* v. *Restall*, [1930] P. 189. In *Robinson* v. *Robinson*, [1943] P. 43 the point was canvassed for the first time that a husband was precluded on the ground of public policy from setting up his wife's adultery in proceedings for maintenance if he had failed to defend the petition on which she obtained a decree and Mr. Justice Henn-Collins decided that the point was a good one. In *Duchesne* v. *Duchesne*, [1951] P. 101 Mr. Justice Pearce had obiter expressed qualified approval of the judgment. But in *Field* v. *Field*, [1964] P. 336 Mr. Justice Wrangham, rightly in his Lordship's view, refused to recognize the existence of any such rule of public policy.
>
> His Lordship was satisfied that today public policy did not require the existence of such a rule and he doubted whether it ever did. He recognised that for better or for worse the public attitude to divorce had undergone profound changes and what

might properly have been recognised as a rule of public policy in 1943 or 1951 was not necessarily valid in 1969.

When a marriage had broken down irretrievably and it was obvious that it would be dissolved, it seemed wrong that a great deal of public time and money should be spent in deciding which of the parties was to be granted the decree or whether perhaps both should be granted a decree. Still less was a respondent obliged to spend time and money in calling evidence as to whether or not facts might exist which might theoretically entitle the court in its discretion to refuse a decree. Everyone knew that until comparatively recently divorce cases had habitually been hotly contested in public at great expense to the parties or to the Legal Aid Fund solely for the purpose of securing a supposed benefit for one or other of the parties in future maintenance or custody proceedings. That could not serve any useful purpose and might even be regarded as contrary to modern concepts of public policy.

In the present case, accordingly, the marriage having irretrievably broken down, the husband was not precluded by any rule of public policy from alleging desertion by his wife when the parties' conduct was being investigated in maintenance proceedings, or from denying allegations made by his wife against him in her discretion statement. The appeal should be allowed.

Lord Justice Edmund Davies, concurring, said that the question of whose conduct actually broke up a marriage was of vital importance in maintenance proceedings, and it would in truth be contrary to public policy were the husband restricted as it had been submitted he should be. *Robinson* v. *Robinson* was wrongly decided.

Sir Gordon Willmer, also concurring, said that the matter was likely to become of increasing importance if and when the new Matrimonial Causes Act came into force. It was likely that when decrees of divorce could be granted on mere proof of breakdown of the marriage, the real disputes between the parties would only emerge in the course of subsequent ancillary proceedings.

In other words, in future, instead of having defended cases where issues were fought out in the open in order to help determine maintenance liabilities and rights, the fight will take place after decree nisi, usually in the privacy of Chambers and the conduct of the parties will be very relevant as it should be. This was made clear by the Lord Chancellor at the Committee stage of the Divorce Reform Bill (*Hansard*: House of Lords, 11 July 1969) when he said: '. . . fault will still be relevant to the custody of the children and in questions of finance.'

Under the Matrimonial Proceedings and Property Act 1970 which tidies up the law relating to financial provision in matrimonial cases, the Court is specifically enjoined to take into account the conduct of the parties. To take into account conduct means judging in terms of guilt and innocence and such judgments will have to be made—and yet one of the main arguments for the introduction of the principle of breakdown is that usually there are faults on both sides and that the whole concept of guilt and innocence is something one wants to get rid of in matrimonial cases.

Mud will therefore still be thrown and it is possible that more mud will be thrown than in the past; that is, there may be far more cases where the parties are inclined to bring up each other's conduct than there would have been—particularly as the result of the case I have just referred to. No longer will a husband have to choose whether to defend his wife's allegations of cruelty, weighing up the cost of a fight in the open in the High Court against the cost of maintaining her—he can let her get her decree and then put his case against her when she claims maintenance. So we will get to the position where a husband is publicly labelled as cruel on the hearing of his wife's Petition whilst some months later he will explain to the Court that he did not defend the charge because the marriage had broken down but he had not really been cruel—in fact it was the other way around.

There may well be, therefore, more litigation than in the past although it will be normally behind closed doors and there will also be increased litigation in the County Court at rates of remuneration which will probably lead to more firms of solicitors refusing to do divorce work particularly in central London where running expenses are so high.

Meanwhile there will also be a tendency for litigation to increase because of the difficulty of advising clients about maintenance to which I have already referred.

Members of the Services, men working for commercial companies and diplomatic staff who are posted abroad and prisoners all have something in common since 1 January 1971. They are living apart from their wives and as the months go by they will be able to add to their other difficulties and frustrations the knowledge that even if they parted on terms of perfect amity with their wives nevertheless the wives can use the time when they are apart to count towards the five years when they can petition. These husbands will have to console themselves with the reflection that their position was discussed in Parliament even though nothing was done about it.

So far as prisoners are concerned Viscount Dilhorne said in the House of Lords on 11 July 1969:

> ... this Bill will add considerably to the sanctions of our criminal law. Whether that is desirable or not is another matter. But I can see great difficulties arising in the courts. They will have to consider whether the passing of a long sentence . . . may lead to the break up of a marriage when it might not have broken up before.

So far as divorce is concerned the new Act in the main abolishes the old absolute and discretionary bars to relief. Connivance has gone as a bar but perhaps will be taken into account when the conduct of the parties is relevant. A husband can encourage his wife to commit adultery and then tell the Court that he finds it intolerable to live with her and if the marriage has broken down and he is believed the Court will be bound to grant a decree. Collusion will vanish save in one of its meanings. Husband and wife can agree to separate and get a divorce in two years' time or they can agree that one shall commit adultery and go for a divorce immediately. The one thing they will not be allowed to do is to pretend to have committed adultery—that is to say to present a false case to the Court—but it is possible that there may be a tendency in the generally looser attitude which will prevail for the false case to increase in number. After all, if the law allows divorce by consent after two years' separation and the parties feel that their marriage is over why wait two years and why not pretend to commit adultery in the unlikely event of adultery in fact not being available? Neither the Petitioner's own adultery nor delay in bringing a Petition will matter.

The Act pays lip service to the principle of reconciliation. Clause 3 provides that:

> (1) Provision shall be made by rules of court for requiring the solicitor acting for a petitioner for divorce to certify whether he has discussed with the petitioner the possibility of a reconciliation

and given him the names and addresses of persons qualified to help effect a reconciliation between parties to a marriage who have become estranged.

(2) If at any stage of proceedings for divorce it appears to the Court that there is a reasonable possibility of a reconciliation between the parties to the marriage, the Court may adjourn the proceedings for such period as it thinks fit to enable attempts to be made to effect such a reconciliation.

I do not think that these provisions will have any effect whatsoever. Under the law before 1 January 1971 solicitors did their best to assist in achieving a reconciliation where this seemed at all possible. I have frequently suggested to clients that they should try the Marriage Guidance Council or asked them whether they have already done so. In many cases as where, for example, husband and wife have been living apart for years it is a waste of time to mention the possibility. I agree with the comments of Lord Craigmyle in the House of Lords on 30 June 1969:

> The unfortunate solicitor who is handling the matter . . . is landed with the job of discussing with the petitioner the possibility of reconciliation. He has to give the petitioner the name and address of, presumably, a marriage counsellor, or someone with that sort of qualification, but that is all. The solicitor is really wasting his time—and that means his client's money—going through a procedure which is written into the Bill and going through it simply and solely because it is written into the Bill. There is nothing in the Bill which obliges the solicitor or the petitioner, let alone the respondent who is an interested party, actually to seek out positive means of discovering what has really gone wrong with the marriage and taking positive steps to put it right. For this reason I consider that the procedure outlined in Clause 3 makes the whole Bill a laughing stock before it is even on the Statute Book.

The ghost of condonation still walks in the new Act which provides that when there has been adultery or cruelty and the parties have thereafter lived together for a period or periods totalling more than six months the adultery shall be and the cruelty may be disregarded by the Court.

Even the strongest supporters of the new Act realized that to force a divorce after a five-year separation on an innocent middle-aged wife was a bit much for some people to stomach.

Provisions were therefore written into the Act in an attempt to reduce the financial hardship to the divorced wife. Under Clause 4 the grant of a decree nisi on that ground may be opposed because 'the dissolution of the marriage will result in grave financial or other hardship to [the petitioner] . . . and that it would in all the circumstances be wrong to dissolve the marriage'. Under Clause 6, after a decree nisi has been granted, because of five years' separation, or by consent after two, the Court may be asked not to make the decree absolute and it is directed not to do so unless it is satisfied—

(a) that the petitioner should not be required to make any financial provision for the respondent; or

(b) that the financial provision made by the respondent is reasonable and fair *or the best that can be made in the circumstances.*

Anxious wives and eager husbands are already wondering about the meaning of these clauses and will have to see how they are interpreted by the Courts in the next few years. My own view is that in the light of the words in my italics the protection for the deserted wife is pretty slender. Sir Jocelyn Simon has said that 'there is likely to be some temptation to try to muffle any wail of intolerable outrage in the closed chambers of distant County Courts'. But won't the position of the wife who is threatened with a five-year divorce be strengthened by the Matrimonial Proceedings and Property Act 1970? Not in the view of the Lord Chancellor who in the House of Lords on 6 November 1969 said:

Nobody, I think, could have taken more trouble repeatedly to make it plain . . . that whatever remedy that could be provided for those subject to the five year clause under the Divorce Reform Act was contained in the Act itself.

Although there have been many arguments in support of a change in the law it would, I think, be fair to summarize them by saying that it was thought that there was a good deal wrong with the existing law, that it is impossible to judge guilt and innocence and that the doctrine of breakdown was more satisfactory all round than the doctrine of the matrimonial offence. We have ended up with a law which preserves the doctrine of the matrimonial offence and engrafts on to it divorce by consent and divorce against the will of a spouse and which regards conduct—that is comparative guilt or innocence—as relevant in financial matters.

One other major factor influenced those in favour of changing the law. It was estimated by the Law Commission that if the five-year clause were made law there were 180,000 illegitimate children who could be legitimated—speaking of them Lord Stow Hill said in the House of Lords on 30 June 1969:

> Born without their consent into a heartless world not above throwing their illegitimacy in their teeth, they at least cannot be accused of seeking to profit by their own wrong. Surely it is better for the lawfully born children also that there should not be that bitterness between their parents which is likely if their mother seeks to hold a halter around her husband's neck which bastardises the issue of his second union.

And making the concluding speech on the Bill in the House of Commons on 17 October 1969 Mr. Leo Abse in his final sentence urged Parliament to pass a Bill 'which will mean that, although there may be many thousands of divorces, after 1st January, 1971, there will be tens of thousands of long-overdue marriages helping to stabilise family life'.

The position of the illegitimate children of stable, illicit unions was certainly a powerful argument for change although all of us are born without our consent into a heartless world. In 1965 in the speech to which I have already referred on p. 153 Sir Jocelyn Simon said:

> I turn then to the next pillar, the pillar of children's welfare. There are two classes of children concerned, and their interests may be contradictory. There are, first, the children of extra-marital unions where one or both of the parents is married to some other person; there are, secondly, the children of marriages. It is the first class of children which is the main concern of those who wish to extend the grounds of divorce so that it is available at the suit of a guilty party. Although the status of illegitimacy is probably today less injurious or degrading than it has been in the past, clearly the interest of such children will be promoted by enabling their parents to marry. Nevertheless, there are counter-considerations. First, to allow remarriage in such circumstances will only benefit those children of irregular unions whose parents have formed or wish to form a stable connection. In trying to

determine the dimensions of the problem, it is therefore misleading to work on the total numbers of illegitimate children. Secondly, of all marriages the class most likely to end in divorce is, statistically, where the previous marriage of one or both spouses has been dissolved. Thirdly, to facilitate the marriage of the parents of children of an irregular union is by no means the only way of benefiting such children; there is still much that we can do to mitigate the disadvantages of the status of illegitimacy. Fourthly, although increased facilities for divorce and remarriage have no doubt meant that some of those born of the extra-marital unions of the spouses concerned have been legitimated, viewing society as a whole greater facilities for divorce have not meant less illegitimacy. On the contrary, in spite of the increasing knowledge and practice of contraception, there has been a startling increase in the number of illegitimate maternities, the rate of which has risen far faster than the legitimate maternity rate during the last few years. This is not, of course, to prove that more facile divorce directly causes illegitimacy. The increase in divorce and the increase in illegitimacy may both be manifestations of one moral malady—a failure in loyalty and compunction in the closest personal relations. But it certainly cannot be excluded that society's ready provision of increased facilities for divorce may indirectly be partly responsible for the increase in illegitimacy, not only by making it appear that lack of loyalty and compunction are of little moral or social consequence, but also by offering the possibility and incentive of marriage to those who contract extra-marital unions. Fifthly, and crucially, to meet the undoubtedly hard case of the child of a stable extra-marital union may be to establish a law which could cause injury not only to the innocent spouse of the first marriage but also to a far more numerous class of children, those of marriages which end in divorce. To quote the sociologist who has made the authoritative study of the unmarried mother and her child, 'If, however, divorce were made easier or allowed at the instance of one partner, whatever the other wished, the stability of many marriages would be undermined and the happiness of many other children—the existing and future children of marriage—imperilled. Nearly every marriage has at least some moments of stress when for a brief while the partners rely almost solely on their vow and intention of permanence and society's insistence that marriage should endure. Many good marriages would founder in the absence of this support.'

The very arguments based on the needs of the children of irregular unions plead still more cogently in favour of the children of present and future marriages which might be dissolved. If children of irregular unions are liable to suffer from the insecurity of their background, how much greater is the peril of those whose secure background is suddenly and irreparably disrupted?

. . . I may, perhaps, be forgiven if I repeat to you what I have said about it before. 'We see them as they appear before us on custody disputes, so often playing off one parent against the other, becoming increasingly insecure, distraught, neurotic, and disorderly. . . . It is sometimes argued that a home broken by divorce is better for a child than a home where the parents are deeply at odds. . . . But . . . it is by no means an infrequent experience of judges sitting in custody jurisdiction that it is at the moment of the break-up of the home that one finds a sudden and alarming deterioration in the child—bad behaviour, speech disorders, plummetting down in class, and similar symptoms. In most of the cases the break-up was preceded by some months of ill-feeling and quarrelling between the two parents; but, unless the parents are more than ordinarily careless of the effect on their children, this period does not seem to do nearly so much damage as the break-up of the family.'

Those who are precluded by the present law from securing a divorce against the wishes of an innocent spouse can canvass and lobby their parliamentary representatives, and their stories are no doubt heart-rending. But the children who may be affected by divorce cannot petition the Legislature with their grievances or plead the injuries that they suffer. Others must do it for them. The pillar of the children's welfare must therefore play an important part in the structure of divorce law reform.

I have ventured in this chapter to make some prophecies as to what may happen as a result of the new Act. I can summarize my views by saying that the old grounds of adultery and cruelty will continue to be used extensively, that the reconciliation provisions will prove ineffective and that it will become more difficult to advise on maintenance so that there may be more and not less litigation. But what will it all be like in practice in this new revolutionary era for those who have decided to end their marriages? I cannot see that the actual procedure of obtaining a divorce is going to be very different from the point of view of the unfortunate wife and husband who are involved in the breakdown of their marriage. One of them and probably both will still have to see a solicitor. In hesitant and half-ashamed sentences the story of unhappiness will come stumbling out. It will still matter who wants the divorce and how quickly, and who is going to remarry. There will still be the hopes of keeping other parties out of the proceedings. There will still be anxiety over what is to happen about the home, furniture and money. Joint bank accounts will have to be closed, wills made or remade, accounts at shops stopped. There will still be serious worries about the effect of the break-up on the children, about custody, access and schooling. There will be all the misery of putting asunder what has been joined together in flesh and blood, in children, home, finances, shared memories and future hopes and plans which must occur whenever the most intimate relationship of all ends, whatever the law may permit or forbid.

There will still be a Petition to the Court, still couched in language too formal and stereotyped to describe adequately the infinite variety of thousands of marriages and the unique quality of each. There will still be defended cases where people deny charges of adultery or oppose the grant of a decree on the ground of five years' separation. There will still be fights over custody and access and battles over finance. There will still be hundreds of cases in the Law Reports as new points are established under the 1969 Act. And many an unhappy wife and husband will still feel that the whole process of sorting out the breakdown of their marriage is nasty, brutish and long.

Some comparatively lucky people—where there is sufficient goodwill, money and intelligence—may be able to arrange directly between themselves the details of a divorce by consent but even they will still have to arrange for a Petition to be filed and join the queue of cases to be heard and wait for another three months after the decree nisi before the decree can be made absolute. But then, if there was sufficient goodwill, it was not impossible to obtain a divorce without bitterness before the 1969 Act.

CONCLUSION

Divorce, in fact, is not the destruction of marriage, but the first condition of its maintenance. A thousand indissoluble marriages mean a thousand marriages and no more. A thousand divorces may mean two thousand marriages; for the couples may marry again. Divorce only re-assorts the couples: a very desirable thing when they are ill-assorted.

GEORGE BERNARD SHAW: From the Preface to *Getting Married*
(1908)

The Enemy's demand on humans takes the form of a dilemma; either complete abstinence, or unmitigated monogamy. . . . We have rendered the former very difficult to them. The latter, for the last few centuries, we have been closing up as a way of escape. We have done this through the poets and novelists by persuading the humans that a curious, and usually short-lived, experience which they call 'being in love' is the only respectable ground for marriage; that marriage can, and ought to, render this excitement permanent; and that a marriage which does not do so is no longer binding . . . thanks to us, the idea of marrying with any other motive seems to them low and cynical. Yes, they think that. They regard the intention of loyalty to a partnership for mutual help, for the preservation of chastity, and for the transmission of life, as something lower than a storm of emotion. (Don't neglect to make your man think the marriage-service very offensive.)

C. S. LEWIS: *The Screwtape Letters* (1942)

Personal attachment is a very happy foundation for friendship; yet, when even two virtuous young people marry, it would perhaps be happy if some circumstances checked their passion; if the recollection of some prior attachment, or disappointed affection, made it on one side, at least, rather a match founded on esteem. In that case they would look beyond the present moment, and try to render the whole of life respectable, by forming a plan to regulate a friendship which only death ought to dissolve.

MARY WOLLSTONECRAFT: *A Vindication of the Rights of Woman*
(1792)

St. Gregory the Great describes the virtue of a priest, who, through motives of piety, had discarded his wife. As he lay dying, she hastened to him to watch the bed which for forty years she had not been allowed to share, and, bending over what seemed the inanimate form of her husband, she tried to ascertain whether any breath still remained, when the dying saint, collecting his last energies, exclaimed, 'Woman, begone; take away the straw; there is fire yet.'

W. E. H. LECKY: *History of European Morals* (1869)

Where did it all go wrong? . . . Marriage is not a permanent fixed structure, outside of, and separate from, the couple who have bought the lease. Divorce is not a kind of malignant burglar who climbs in through the lavatory window to break up the home, or another woman who is deposited on the doorstep by inertia selling or a monster from outer space which rips off the roof with his knuckles as he takes a short cut through the neighbourhood. Marriage is not an 'it'.

It is you, or (more accurately) us, or (more probably) me, who should be blamed.

ALAN BRIEN: *New Statesman*, 9 January 1970

One fine morning last month Marriage in England was suddenly abolished.

Nineteenth Century Magazine, May 1891

Like many other people I got married in a church and although I was in a bit of a daze at the time I understood the words of the marriage service and sincerely intended to try to put into practice those wonderful words 'for better for worse, for richer for poorer, in sickness and in health, to love and to cherish, till death us do part . . .' and yet—and yet if I had had to put up with what some of my clients have had to put up with for years, my marriage would not have lasted six months. I should have walked out. There is an infinity of ways in which one spouse can be cruel to another and some of the cruellest are not the easiest to put into words.

> Yet each man kills the thing he loves,
> By each let this be heard,
> Some do it with a bitter look,
> Some with a flattering word,
> The coward does it with a kiss,
> The brave man with a sword!
>
> Some kill their love when they are young,
> And some when they are old;
> Some strangle with the hands of lust,
> Some with the hands of gold;
> The kindest use a knife because
> The dead so soon grow cold.

I do not subscribe to the current fashion of thought which has led to the enshrining of the principle of breakdown in an Act of Parliament in a half-hearted attempt to get rid of the matrimonial offence. In the words of the Bishop of Leicester in the House of Lords on 30 June 1969:

> I am not myself entirely converted to this idea of the breakdown of marriage as the principal ground for divorce. This idea has swept through the thoughtful world almost like an epidemic.

The Law Commission in their Working Paper No. 9 on Family Law in April 1967 said:

> But it is now generally recognised that on the breakdown of marriages there are usually faults on both sides and that it is often impossible with justice to stigmatise one as 'guilty' and the other as 'innocent'.

I agree that there are often faults on both sides but I believe that in many cases if all the facts were known most people would say that far more of the fault was on one side than the other. The husband who leaves his middle-aged wife for a younger woman can sometimes persuade his mistress and himself that he has been suffering under his wife's faults for years but he frequently only abandons her when her sexual attractions have faded.

I realize that in some cases the commission of the matrimonial offence may be the symptom of the breakdown but in my experience the marriage in many cases does not break down because of incompatibility which prompts the matrimonial offence but because one party is more selfish than the other and as part of his or her selfishness is unkind or cruel or commits adultery or deserts.

So far as adultery is concerned I have always felt that what matters far more than the adultery is the breach of trust which is usually involved. I can't see how a marriage can function without trust whether it be in frankness and co-operation over the family finances or sexual fidelity. Affection and kindness, sexual compatibility, shared love of children, all these are obviously very important, but without trust none of them can survive for long. And though one may kiss and make up after some quarrels and a short separation, I do not understand how even if one spouse forgives the other's adultery, trust can usually be re-established.

So despite my marriage vows I have found no difficulty of conscience in acting as a divorce lawyer for all these years. I am in favour of divorce on the grounds established by A. P. Herbert's Act in 1937. I am also in favour of divorce by consent and spoke publicly in support of it years ago. Anything which enables people to bring their marriages to an end without bitterness or the public washing of dirty linen is to the good. Or as Milton put it:

> . . . it is a less breach of wedlock to part with wise and quiet consent betimes, than still to fail and profane that mystery of joy and union with a polluting sadness and perpetual distemper: for it is not the outward continuing of marriage that keeps whole that covenant, but whatsoever does most according to peace and love, whether in marriage or in divorce. . . .

Nor do I think that because divorce by consent is available people will rush off to the Divorce Court after a slight tiff. In my experience most people take their marriages very seriously and are most upset at the prospect of breakdown. It is not the most enjoyable part of my work to comfort weeping clients— women and sometimes men.

During the long debates which have taken place over the Divorce Reform Act no one has spoken more strongly against it than Lady Summerskill. In her campaign against the Bill she described it as a 'Casanova's Charter'. It was a mistake. It enabled her opponents to point out, correctly, that Casanovas do not need charters. Indeed the Act may have the opposite effect. Until January 1971 husbands have been able to set up a mistress and then plead to the mistress that unfortunately their wives will not give them a divorce. In future they may find themselves out of the frying-pan of the first marriage into the fire of the second.

What sticks in my gullet is divorce after five years' separation against the will of the deserted spouse and in saying that I am not forgetting the stable illicit unions which may result in marriage or the many children who will achieve legitimacy as a result of the Divorce Reform Act. But so far as the five-year provision is concerned I cannot do better to express my feelings than to quote the words of a former Lord Chancellor of England, Viscount Simonds, who in the House of Lords on 10 July 1969 during the Committee stage of the Divorce Reform Bill, said:

> May I say just a few words? I had not intended to speak, indeed, it is a very long time since I addressed your Lordships, I am not only old-fashioned—and therefore, I am afraid, will earn the noble Baroness's disapproval—but I am also very old, and I had little thought of ever addressing your Lordships again. But this is a unique occasion, unique in this: that this Bill not only makes a great change in a most important part of our social law—of that, I think there is no doubt—but it also does what no other measure that I, in the course of a quarter of a century in this House, have ever heard before. It patently and I think avowedly does grave injustice to many individual human beings. It is for that reason that I venture to rise.
>
> I wonder whether I could bring to your Lordships' minds as vividly as possible the simple issue which arises between two human beings who have somehow gone astray and are, both of them probably, certainly one of them, in sore distress. I would ask your Lordships to regard yourselves, each one of you, as a judge before whom a case of this kind comes. These cases are, of course, of infinite variety, but I will take a simple case and will ask your Lordships to imagine that you are sitting as a judge, dedicated as you of course are to the administration of justice according to law; and according to law, if this measure passes unamended—as God forbid!—then this is the sort of case you will meet.
>
> A man (or it may be a woman; the sex does not matter) will come before you claiming a divorce from the other spouse. You ask that man, 'What is the ground upon which you claim a dissolution of your marriage?' He says, 'My marriage has irretrievably broken down.' You say, 'Upon what ground?' He says 'For five years my wife and I have been living apart.' You say to him, 'Well, how did that come about?' He says, 'Well, it was in the year 1960 that I married my wife. She was young and rather inexperienced. She bore our child and she nourished it. She looked after me and my house and home. But, poor wretch she got very dull and tired, and I got bored. So in the year 1963 I left her. Since then, we have been living apart, I sometimes alone, sometimes with another woman. She has asked me to go back. Quite

recently she asked me to go back, saying that our son had now reached an age at which he needed the care and guidance of a father. But I have refused, and you will see, therefore, that the marriage has irretrievably broken down; and it cannot be denied that I have done the best I can to break it down irretrievably.'

That is the case that a judge will have to hear and . . . I think you would get hot under the collar and you would say, 'You have done grievous wrong to this woman, and now you seek the benefit of the wrong you have done and ask for the dissolution of your marriage.' To which he will answer, 'But in the House of Lords, this question of getting the benefit of your wrong was raised and discussed, and the noble Lord who introduced the Bill said that the principle that a man should not get the benefit of his own wrong was really senseless. . . .'

I cannot understand any man whose conscience is not affected by such a consideration and who would not say, 'I will not vote for a measure which has that result', unless indeed he has reached a stage of civilisation and passed from that to a stage of decadence.

It is upon the ground of the injustice which this Bill will do to individuals that I oppose it. . . . I would beg your Lordships to follow the pattern of justice, decency and honour, and refuse to the man who comes before you the benefit of his own wrong.

Quite apart from any question of injustice, far too little account has been taken in my view of the effect of the five years' separation provision on those wives who are willing to divorce their husbands and this effect was already being felt even before the Act was passed. Before this, how much maintenance an innocent wife got was determined by the interrelationship of the following factors:

(1) the means of the parties;
(2) the principles on which the Court grants maintenance;
(3) the conduct of the parties;
(4) which party wants the divorce.

If an innocent wife is provided by her husband with unimpeachable evidence of his adultery and a request for a divorce and she is herself not anxious for a divorce but reluctantly decides to let him have his freedom, she may well end up with more furniture, a better home, more maintenance and more security, than a wife who is anxious to divorce a husband who does not want to be divorced. The Court will not allow the former wife to use her position as one of blackmail to enforce an extortionate claim but the possible limits of financial provision being so vague there is room for a good deal of manœuvre in negotiations between solicitors. In future, however, the wife's bargaining position will be weakened because she will know that the husband can always fall back on the five years' separation provision. It is true that this, in the main, will affect middle-aged wives whose husbands earn a substantial income and have other assets but there are still quite a number of such wives whose marriages break up.

Meanwhile, there has been a great change in the public's attitude to divorce since the days of Dilke and Parnell. The former was prevented from again becoming a Minister of the Crown. Of the latter's case R. C. K. Ensor wrote: 'on 17th November 1890 the Divorce Court granted a decree nisi to Captain O'Shea in a suit against his wife, in which Parnell was the co-respondent. There was no defence . . . on the following day the National Liberal Federation met at Sheffield; and though nothing was said in public, it was privately represented to the front bench in the persons of Morley and Harcourt that English non-conformists could not continue any association with the Irish party unless it changed its leader. This line was quite a sincere and natural one for religious Victorians to take.' Writing of 1922, A. J. P. Taylor said:

Divorce remained a serious barrier in public life and, in Court circles, an insuperable one. Riddell, a newspaper proprietor, was the first 'guilty' party in a divorce suit to be made a peer, after ineffective protests from George V; Josiah Wedgwood the first to sit in a cabinet (the Labour Government of 1924). These were isolated cases, and the Conservative party maintained a ban on divorce until after the Second World War.

Speaking of the 1936 Abdication crisis he wrote:

Members of Parliament, visiting their constituencies at the week-end, learnt the strong feeling against Edward, particularly, it is said, in the north of England. No doubt the feeling was all the stronger from the suddenness with which the news had been sprung on the public as happened with Parnell long before.

But the feeling was not strong enough to prevent A. P. Herbert getting his Bill through in the following year. Now we have reached the stage when Members of both front benches can go through the Divorce Courts without that in itself imperilling their careers, although, as recently as 1955, the fact that Group Captain Peter Townsend's marriage had ended in divorce influenced Princess Margaret's decision not to marry him. In her personal message she specifically referred to 'the Church's teaching that Christian marriage is indissoluble'.

Divorce then has become socially acceptable—almost, one might say, if the word were still fashionable or, indeed, applicable at all in this day and age, respectable. Neighbours pry less into the matrimonial history of their neighbours and if, for some reason, divorce is not immediately available, a change of name by deed poll will, for a time at least, cover a multitude of socially ambiguous situations. It is understood that anyone's marriage may fail and it is also understood that the party labelled 'guilty' in Court is not necessarily the guiltier one in fact. Indeed so well is the latter point understood that someone who has been really guilty may escape social censure because the guilty are thought to be not necessarily guilty.

But perhaps to go through the Divorce Courts more than once, unless one belongs to a very select group of occupations—mainly in the entertainment world—is not quite so socially acceptable. It indicates, maybe, a degree of accident-proneness that leads neighbours to adopt a slightly cautious attitude. So that the man who has abandoned his first, middle-aged wife for a second younger charmer may not commonly repeat the process. In any event if his second wife is sufficiently younger than he, her charms may last him out. As Aristotle said: 'Women should marry whey they are about eighteen years of age and men at seven-and-thirty; then they are in the prime of life, and the decline in the powers of both will coincide.'

Apart from the possibility of social disapproval and the probability that for most men the second younger wife will last him out, the cost of maintaining three wives will probably keep the number of second divorces low although of all marriages, second marriages are statistically the most likely to end in divorce.

Speaking in the House of Lords on 24 June 1937 during the debate on the Herbert Bill the Archbishop of Canterbury said 'that the danger may be, not the dissolution of individual marriages, but of the gradual dissolution of the institution of marriage itself'. Have we now reached that stage?

Within the space of a few weeks in the autumn of 1969 Mr. Malcolm Muggeridge chaired a programme on TV which discussed 'Why Marriage?' Mr. Arthur Koestler in *The Times* foresaw that to go through two or three marriages in a lifetime would be considered the norm, facilitated through divorce by consent. 'The family unit will be preserved, but premarital and extramarital affairs will be taken for granted.' Dr. Helena Wright recommended that marriage partners should have outside affairs provided they were honest with each other about what they were doing. Miss Katharine Whitehorn in the *Observer*, echoing the views of Bertrand Russell expressed forty years earlier, was asking why women's equality should not mean that wives also 'could have a bit on the side, as in the French system, without cracking the family set-up from which older women and younger children get so much. It might', in her view, 'be a lot nearer to what women really want than the shifting sands of easy divorce.'

Mr. Jim Radford in *Help* advocated 'flexibility and experiment, trial group marriages and communal households'. He said: 'The most practical (sic) and attractive arrangement to my mind, would involve five or six couples with love and respect for each other, living together with income and children in common.' The *Evening Standard* reported that 'nearly half the adult population—and a big majority of all those under forty-five—now favour unmarried girls being able to obtain the Pill'. *The Times* informed us that a contraceptive machine was to be installed at Leeds University 'in an effort to decrease the number of unwanted pregnancies. During the 1967–68 academic year 49 unmarried girl students became pregnant.'

In January 1970 Mr. Alistair Service who organized campaigns to support the Divorce Reform Act of 1969, writing in the Journal of the National Marriage Guidance Council, expressed the view that a reduction to one year's separation for divorce by consent might be 'found desirable after our new law has been working for a few years'. He also forecast that 'either it will become perfectly acceptable at all levels of society that the young live together unmarried or else a divorce in the mid-twenties will become accepted as a perfectly ordinary part of life'.

What is the country coming to? Trial marriage, premarital and extramarital intercourse for men and women, group marriage and consecutive monogamy all are described, prescribed or prophesied in the above quoted passages. What is the country coming to?

> The nation was out of health. It passed through a phase like an adolescence; its temper was explosive and quarrelsome. . . . Whole classes or strata of society were, in some degree, tasting power for the first time; and as they pushed their way out of the inarticulate and into the articulate part of the community, a kind of upstart arrogance became vocal with them. In religion, in social relations, in politics, in business, men grown contemptuous of the old ideals were stridently asserting new ones. The former clear objectives were gone, and as yet nothing took their place. Those . . . concerned with the fashionable surface of life and letters in London are struck by the revulsion from puritanism to raffishness—the epoch . . . of a more flaunting West End vice . . . Very certainly it was a period of widening comfort; . . . of relaxation in taboos both social and moral; of growing mental freedom, accompanied, however, by a loss of concentration and direction.

Poor old England, having lost an Empire and not found a role, reeling from the hangover of the permissive sixties into the uncertainties of the seventies. In fact it is R. C. K. Ensor commenting on the last ten years of Victoria's reign when the Empire was at its height. A few years later, at a time when the force of the non-conformist vote was at its strongest, Queen Alexandra invited her husband's mistress into her home and the Lord Chief Justice giving evidence before the Gorell Commission commented on 'the terrible extent to which immorality' existed between boys and girls from the ages of fourteen to eighteen.

But surely nothing can be more disgusting than the orgies in which some of the young have recently been indulging.

> At Christmas I went to stay at ————, where there was a large party. ———— was there, and read the marriage service over two dogs, ending 'whom man hath joined, let not dog put asunder'.

The writer, Bertrand Russell; the time, 1915; the place, Garsington; the 'priest', Keynes; the witnesses amongst others, Lytton Strachey, Katherine Mansfield and Middleton Murry. As to lifelong monogamy Lecky wrote in 1869:

> We can prove that it is on the whole most conducive to the happiness, and also to the moral elevation, of all parties. But beyond this point it would, I conceive, be impossible to advance, except by the assistance of a special revelation. It by no means follows that because this should be the dominant type it should be the only one, or that the interests of society demand that all connections should be forced into the same die. Connections, which were confessedly only for a few years, have always subsisted side by side with permanent marriages; and in periods when public opinion, acquiescing in their propriety, inflicts no excommunication on one or both partners, when these partners are not living the demoralising and degrading life which accompanies the consciousness of guilt, and when proper provision is made for the children who are born, it would be, I believe, impossible to prove, by the light of simple and unassisted reason, that such connections should be invariably condemned. It is extremely important, both for the happiness and for the moral well-being of men, that life-long unions should not be effected simply under the imperious prompting of a blind appetite.

So far as prostitution and premarital intercourse go the following passage has a contemporary ring:

> I am afraid, as respects the gross evils of prostitution, that there is hardly any country in the world where they prevail to a greater extent than in our own. With regard to another most dangerous evil—namely, what is called antenuptial incontinence, its prevalence is so general in country as well as in town, that we must all feel humbled to the dust when we consider with how little strictness Christian obligations are in that respect observed.

It comes from a speech on 31 July 1857 by Gladstone. Thirty years later Thomas Hardy in *Jude the Obscure* took premarital sexual intercourse as the accepted thing in Wessex—'under the hedge which divided the field from a distant plantation girls had given themselves to lovers who would not turn their heads to look at them by the next harvest'.

As for pornography . . . 'Have not all the abominations of the public stews been opened to view by lewd pictures exposed to sale at noon-day? Have not histories of romances of the vilest prostitutes been published, intended merely to display the most execrable scenes of lewdness; lewdness represented without disguise, and nothing omitted that might inflame the corrupt passions of the youth of the nation. What was the encouragement for men to dare giving such an affront not only to the common sense but to the common law of the country? Was it not the quick sale that these pictures and these books had?' So wrote Bishop Sherlock in a letter to his diocese in 1750.

Perhaps modern views on marriage, of which I have given a selection, are not so much important because of the unknown number of people who hold them but because they have been and are being expressed publicly for the first time and in an increasing volume.

Will the ever increasing length of life itself impose an intolerable strain on lifelong monogamy? Will men welcome spare parts transplanted into an old wife or will they prefer to swap for an entirely new model?

It certainly looks as though marriage is in a poor state of health—until one reflects that today people can't wait to marry, they marry younger, they remarry the day after the decree nisi has been made absolute and they are queuing up in numbers to marry under the new Act having lived with the other man or woman for five, ten, fifteen and twenty years— but they still want to marry before they die.

In view of the difficulties which modern marriage has to contend with, it seems to me to be in a fairly healthy state and I ought to have a jaundiced view as a divorce lawyer. I always seem to be sending silver wedding greetings to my friends and the truth is that marriage is much more difficult now than it was a hundred years ago. A partnership is a much more delicate relationship than a dictatorship with father as boss of the family. Despite this, nine out of ten marriages do not end in the Divorce Court. In the words of the Law Commission— 'The number of divorces has, of course, risen much more rapidly than the married population but this . . . is not necessarily an indication of an increase in the proportion of broken homes. It is almost certain that it is very largely due to the readier availability of divorce rather than to an increase in the proportion of marriages which break down.' It may be that a marriage which can be ended, after three years of marriage and two years' separation, simply by agreement is not the same kind of marriage in which I asked my wife to join me twenty-three years ago. But perhaps it is better. The most famous definition of marriage in English law states that it must be a 'voluntary union for life of one man and one woman, to the exclusion of all others'. In the past the word 'voluntary' has been taken to refer to the inception of the marriage. One of the reasons I like divorce by consent is that for the vast majority of those whose marriages do not end in divorce it emphasizes the voluntary nature of the continuing bond.

If we are worried about the increase in divorce statistics it is as well to remember the words of the Bishop of Durham who also spoke in the House of Lords on 24 June 1937:

> If the number of divorces were a safe indication of social morals it were indeed possible to make the whole community pure at a stroke by prohibiting divorce.

Meanwhile there has been a general improvement in women's position. Before marriage a woman can achieve financial independence and even during marriage an increasing number of wives are not solely dependent on whatever allowance their husbands choose to make them. During marriage they rightly expect to be treated as partners and contraception enables them to control the size of their families. If the marriage fails, they have equal rights to divorce and gradually improving property and maintenance rights after divorce. If their children are young and they have been good mothers they will almost certainly get at least care and control of the children—i.e. physical custody of them—irrespective of how badly they may have behaved as wives.

Why then do I have a persistent feeling that the status of wives as a whole in marriage has been weakened? The fact is that many of the apparent improvements in women's rights have led to a general deterioration in the security of marriage from the point of view of the middle-aged wife.

N

Because women are free to go out to work they inevitably associate with men and association breeds interest and tends to seek opportunity. Because even a guilty wife will probably keep her children, a wife can safely abandon her husband and break up another marriage. Because of the free use of contraceptives the restraint on sexual intercourse outside the marriage has been removed. Because claims for damages for adultery are abolished a deterrent to the break-up of marriage is removed. Because it is fashionable to say that there is no such thing as guilt or innocence the social stigma of divorce is lessened for the one who wants to break up the marriage. Because women can go out to work the amount of maintenance which a husband will have to pay to his former wife will take account of her earning capacity and if she is capable of working his liability will decrease. Because women can go out to work the mistress can and does contribute to the upkeep of the second home which might otherwise be too much of a burden to the husband. Because young women will live with older men there is a constant threat to the middle-aged woman and for many her fate has been sealed by the provision which now enables the younger woman to compel the husband to go for a divorce after five years' separation. This is the paradox to which I referred in my introduction. One of the so far inescapable, if unpleasant facts of life, is that there are far more young women prepared to set up home with older men (whether married or not) than there are young men prepared to set up home with older women. One hundred and twelve years after divorce first became available in a court of law, women's well-justified struggle for equality has now ended in a situation where a divorce can be forced on an innocent wife against her will after years of marriage. A well-meaning attempt to help illegitimate children has put the young mistress in a stronger position than the old wife, although in her turn the young mistress will become an old wife.

It is an odd end to an odd story since the more one considers the history of divorce in England the more curious it becomes. It seems strange that in England it was more difficult to end a marriage after than before the Reformation; that Scotland should have accepted divorce on the grounds of adultery and desertion centuries before England; that the first major step towards divorce in England should have been debated during the Crimean War and the Indian Mutiny and the Act passed when the religious and social climate of Victorian England might have been expected to be strongly opposed to it; that A. P. Herbert succeeded in getting his Bill through although several others before him had failed and the Abdication Crisis occurred when the Bill was in Committee; that after decades of struggle for equal rights for women the 1969 Act should have allowed divorce against the will of an innocent wife with hardly a whisper of protest from the middle-aged daughters of the suffragettes. I cannot help thinking that the champions of women's rights have been asleep during the past few years and will wake to find that the male has won the last battle in a hundred years' war.

APPENDIX A

TO THE RIGHT HONOURABLE THE LORDS
ASSEMBLED IN PARLIAMENT

THE HUMBLE PETITION OF ANN ROOS THE WIFE OF JOHN LORD ROOS

SHEWETH

That your petitioner upon diverse and barbarous cruelties from the Lord Roos her Husband, comenced an Action against him in the Court of Arches for Alimony to avoid which the said Lord Roos by the Impetuous instigation and abounding malice of his Lady Mother the Countess of Rutland contrived a most false and Scandalous Accusation of Adultery against your Petitioner in the said Court of Arches, and by corrupt practices and perjuries and Subornations of Witnesses obtained a sentence of divorce a mensa et thoro against your Petitioner.

That your Petitioner having very little or noe maintenance to support herself became Indebted to several persons who by the severe practices of the said Countess of Rutland, and the said Lord Roos, endeavoured to arrest your Petitioner and to commit her to prison, that thereby your Petitioner should be disabled to attend her cause in the said Court of Arches.

That your Petitioner upon this violent and barbarous Prosecution, was forced to fly into Ireland to preserve herselfe from Prison in England whereby she was Rendered Incapable to defend herself or instruct her Counsell And soe sentence passed against your Petitioner in her absence.

That your Petitioner hath addressed herself by Petition to his Most Sacred Majesty to be restored to the benefit of an appeal to prosequit her just defence in a legall way.

That the late act of Parliament to illegitimate her sonnes begotten by the said Lord Roos and to dispoil your Petitioner of her Honnour passed your Petitioner not being Summoned, heard, or defended.

That the bill now presented to your Lordships on the behalf of the said Lord Roos her Husband to be divorced a vinculo matrimonii is the most unexampled bill that ever in this kind was offered to the Parliament of England.

That there is noe president of a parliament that ever yett authorised and licensed a divorce a vinculo matrimonii whatever there has been to tolerate the same unjustly ex post facto.

That hitherto all sentences of divorce in the Ecclesiasticall Courts of this Kingdom for Adultery conteine in the body of the said Sentences expresse Inhibitions to the parties not to marry againe, till one of the Parties be dead and the like Inhibition is made in the very Sentence of divorce upon which the said Lord Roos grounds his bill presented to this Honourable House.

Your Petitioner humbly Prayeth that since the said Sentence in the Arches Court was grounded upon the perjuries and Subornations of witnesses obtained in her absence, and undefended that your Petitioner had neither bread to keepe her from starving, nor moneys to defend herselfe but was by the Insolent power of the said Countess of Rutland and the cruelties of her husband reduced to extreame misery and poverty of which soe cruell advantage was taken by them, to pursue your Petitioner though unheard, to dishonour, And her children to bastardize and considering that the proofes of the said perjuries subornations and corrupt practices, by undenyable Testimonies lately come to your Petitioners knowledge, may before Commissioners of appeale be made apparent if his Most Excellent Majesty shall be graciously pleased to graunt a Commission to examine the meritts of her cause and your Petitioner be allowed monyes as is usual in such cases, To retaine Counsell for her just defence And considering that the said bill, carries not onely the particular dishonnour and transsendent Injury to your Petitioner but may Influence a fatal and universall Inconvenience upon all the families in the Kingdom That your Lordships would be pleased to attend the issue of your Petitioners appeal now depending before his Most

Excellent Majesty whereby your Petitioner doubts not to make her Innocence appear clearly And the fraudes calumny and Inhuman cruelties of the said Countess and Lord Roos Evident to the whole Kingdom.

And your Petitioner shall ever pray etc.

Anne Roos

APPENDIX B

No. 3419

IN THE HIGH COURT OF JUSTICE

PROBATE DIVORCE AND ADMIRALTY DIVISION

DIVORCE

O'SHEA   V   O'SHEA   and   PARNELL
(William Henry)   (Katharine)   (Charles Stewart)

THE following are the further and better particulars (in substitution for or in addition to the particulars filed in July 1890) of the allegations contained in paragraphs 2, 3, 4, 5, and 7 of the Answer of the Respondent filed in this Suit and furnished pursuant to the order dated the 9th day of June 1890.

1. THE further particulars in reference to the allegations contained in paragraph 2 of the said answer are as follows:—

THE Petitioner constantly connived at and was accessory to the said alleged adultery from the autumn of the year 1880 to the Spring of the year 1886 inclusive by inducing directing and requiring the Respondent to form the acquaintance of the Co-respondent and to see him alone and to ask favors of him in the interest and for the advantage of the Petitioner both before and after he had accused her of misconduct and adultery with the Co-respondent by directing the Respondent to invite the Co-respondent to her house and to ask favors of him in the absence of the Petitioner in his interest and for his advantage both before and after he had accused her of adultery with the Co-respondent by his knowledge that the Co-respondent was constantly at the house of the Respondent in the Petitioners absence and by leaving the Co-respondent alone at Wonersh Lodge with the Respondent on most of those occasions when the Petitioner left to go to London or elsewhere both before and after he had accused her of misconduct and adultery with the Co-respondent

2. THE Petitioner also constantly connived at and was accessory to the said alleged adultery by asking favors of the Co-respondent for his the Petitioners advantage and profit both

184

before and after he had accused the Respondent of misconduct and adultery with the Co-respondent

3. THE Petitioner also constantly connived at and was accessory to the said alleged adultery after he had accused the Respondent of misconduct and adultery with the Co-respondent by constantly seeking to intimidate the Respondent, and to compel and induce her to make fraudulent misrepresentations as to the influence of the Petitioner and as to her influence over the Co-respondent for the advantage and profit of the Petitioner.

4. THE Petitioner also connived at and was accessory to the said alleged adultery both before and after he had accused the Respondent of misconduct and adultery with the Co-respondent by trafficking and attempting to traffic in her and his alleged influence over the Co-respondent for his the Petitioner's advantage and profit.

5. THE Petitioner also connived at and was accessory to the said alleged adultery after he had accused the Respondent of misconduct and adultery with the Co-respondent by constantly seeking to intimidate the Respondent and to compel and induce her to apply to her Aunt, the late Mrs. Benjamin Wood, for large sums of money for his purposes under the pretext that such sums were required for the use and benefit of the Respondent and her children; and by intimidation compelling and inducing the Respondent to make a fraudulent application to Sir Thomas Barrett Lennard and Charles Page Wood for a portion of a trust fund held by them in trust for other purposes, so that the Petitioner might misappropriate such portion of the said fund for his own purposes.

6. THE Petitioner first accused the Respondent of adultery with the Co-respondent in 1881 and many times since, and he also frequently stated that he was not the father of the three last born children, but that the Co-respondent was their father, and he made these accusations and statements for the purpose of intimidating the Respondent as aforesaid and otherwise as hereafter stated.

7. THE further particulars in reference to paragraph 3 of the said answer are as follows:—

THE Petitioner has been constantly guilty of neglect and misconduct since the marriage by wilfully absenting himself living apart and separating himself from the Respondent as mentioned in paragraph 8 of these particulars by habitual intemperance by neglecting to contribute anything for the maintenance and support of the Respondent and her children by depriving the Respondent of money which she had received from her relations for the maintenance and support of herself and children and using it for his own purposes by squandering his means in betting on horse racing and by rash speculations. By directing her to see divers persons alone in his interest and for his advantage. And further the Petitioners (sic) was also guilty of the neglect and misconduct as alleged in the particulars given in paragraphs one, two, three, four, five and six hereof

8. THE further particulars in reference to paragraph 4 of the said answer are as follows:

THE Petitioner has habitually separated himself and lived apart from the Respondent without reasonable excuse for long periods during the years 1868, 1869, and 1870, and during the years 1871 and 1872 for a part of the year 1875 during the years 1876 and the years following and wilfully deserted the Respondent without reasonable cause from the Autumn of the year 1884 down to and inclusive of the year 1800.

9. THE further particulars in reference to paragraph 5 of the said answer are as follows:—

THE Petitioner committed adultery in the Spring of 1874 in Paris, with Thérèse Dubuisson and Marie Grande.

IN the summer of 1874 at 100 Buckingham Palace Road, London with the aforesaid Therese Dubuisson and Marie Grande.

IN the year 1875, at Mortlake, with Sarah Winrow the Parlor Maid employed at the house where the Petitioner resided with the Respondent.

IN 1877 and 1878, at Las Minas, Hellin, Spain, with Maria Dominquez.

IN the year 1881, on the 5th April, at No. 16 Charles Street, Haymarket, London, with a prostitute whose name is at present unknown to the Respondent.

IN May 1881, at the same place with Mrs. Deerehurst, and in July with Louisa Leyton.

IN the year 1881, on or about the 13th July at James Street, London, with Mrs. Anna Caroline Steel.

IN March 1882 at 1 Albert Mansions, S.W. with divers prostitutes, whose names are at present unknown to the Respondent.

IN June, 1882, in Paris, with Elise Guérin.

IN November, 1884, at 1 Albert Mansions, S.W. with Rosa Terrice or Tueski.

In February 1885, at Madrid with Amelia Villarde.

IN March or April, 1885, in Madrid, with divers prostitutes whose names are at present unknown to the Respondent.

10. THE further particulars in reference to the allegations contained in paragraph 7 of the said answer are as follows:

THE Petitioner was guilty of cruelty by assaulting the Respondent on or about the 12th day of July 1881 when she was pregnant and by frequently asserting that he the Petitioner was not the Father of her the Respondents last born three children but that the Co-respondent was for the purpose of vexing and annoying the Respondent and injuring her health. And for the same purpose constantly indicated in a variety of ways that he did not consider himself to be the father of the last born three children, but that the Co-respondent was, and the Petitioner habitually neglected the said children and commonly ignored their existence, and was further guilty of the cruelty described in paragraphs 2, 3, 4, 5 and 6 of these particulars.

BIBLIOGRAPHY

ABEL-SMITH, Brian, and STEVENS, Robert: *Lawyers and the Courts*. Heinemann, London, 1967.

ANON: *An Answer to a Book Intituled the Doctrine and Discipline of Divorce*. 1644.

ANON: *Plea for Alteration of the Divorce Laws*. 1831.

ANON: *What will the commons do with the Divorce Bill*. By 'a wife and mother'. 1856.

A BARRISTER: *The Lady's Cabinet Lawyer*. 1837.

BIRKENHEAD, Lord: *Famous Trials*.

BROWNLIE, A. R.: *Blood and the Blood Groups*. 1965.

BURNET, G.: *Bishop Burnet's History of His Own Time*. Thos. Ward, London, 1724.

BURNET, G.: *Is a woman's barrenness a just ground for divorce or for polygamy?* and *Is polygamy in any case lawful under the Gospel?* 1733.

CAMPBELL, Lord: *Life of Lord Campbell*. Ed. by Mrs. Hardcastle. 1881.

COOTE, H. C.: *The Practice of the Ecclesiastical Courts*. Henry Butterworth, London, 1847.

DRYSDALE, Dr. George: *The Elements of Social Science; Physical, Sexual and Natural Religion*. 1855.

EARENGEY, W. G.: *Woman under the Law*. London, 1916.

ENSOR, R. C. K.: *England 1870–1914*. Oxford University Press, 1936.

FELLOWS, Alfred: *The Case against the English Divorce Law*. John Lane, London, 1932.

FLETCHER, Ronald: *Britain in the Sixties—The Family and Marriage*. Penguin, 1962.

GARDINER, Gerald and MARTIN, Andrew: *Law Reform Now!* Gollancz, London, 1963.

GIBBON, Edward: *Decline and Fall of the Roman Empire*. 1776–1788.

GORER, Geoffrey: *Exploring English Character*. Cresset, London, 1955.

GORER, Geoffrey: The *Sunday Times* Report on Sex and Marriage. 1970.

GRAVESON, R. H. and CRANE, F. R.: *A Century of Family Law, 1857–1957*. Sweet & Maxwell, London, 1957.

HALSBURY: *Laws of England*. (3rd Edition.)

Hansard.

HARRISON, Henry: *Parnell Vindicated. The lifting of the veil.* Constable, London, 1931.

HARVEY, C. P.: *On the State of the Divorce Market.* 1953.

HARVEY, C. P.: *The Advocate's Devil.* Stevens, London, 1958.

HASLIP, Joan: *Parnell; A biography.* Cobden-Sanderson, London, 1936.

HERBERT, A. P.: *Holy Deadlock.* Methuen, London, 1934.

HERBERT, A. P.: *The Ayes Have It. The Story of the Marriage Bill.* Methuen, London, 1937.

HEREN, Alistair: *Towards a Quaker View of Sex.* 1963.

INDERWICK, F. A.: *The Divorce and Matrimonial Causes Acts.* London, 1862.

JACKSON, Joseph: *The Formation and Annulment of Marriage.* 1969. (2nd Edition.)

JACQUES, J. W. F.: *Women: and the Unfair position they occupy at the present time.* 1911.

JENKINS, Roy: *Sir Charles Dilke—A Victorian Tragedy.* Collins, 1958.

JOURNALS OF THE HOUSE OF LORDS.

KITCHIN, S. B.: *A History of Divorce.* Chapman and Hall, London, 1912.

THE *Law Reports* AND *Weekly Law Reports.*

THE LAW COMMISSION:

Annual Reports.

Reform of the Grounds of Divorce. The Field of Choice. 1966.

Family Law—Reports on Financial Provision in Matrimonial Proceedings. 1969.

Proposal for abolition of The Matrimonial Remedy of Restitution of Conjugal Rights. 1969.

Breach of Promise of Marriage. 1969.

Working Papers:

No. 9 *Family Law—Matrimonial and Related Proceedings—financial relief.* 1967.

No. 12 *Family Law—Proof of Paternity in civil proceedings.* 1967.

No. 15 *Family Law—Arrangements for the care and upbringing of Children (Section 33 of the Matrimonial Causes Act 1965).* 1968.

No. 20 *Family Law—Nullity of Marriage.* 1968.

No. 21 *Polygamous Marriages.* 1968.

No. 28 *Family Law—Jurisdiction in Matrimonial Causes (other than Nullity).* 1970.

LATIMER, Hugh: *A most faithful sermon preached before the King's most excellent majesty and his most honourable council, in Court at Westminster, by the Reverend Father Master Hugh Latimer, (in Lent) anno domini 1550.*

LECKY, W. E. H. *History of European Morals from Augustus to Charlemagne.* Longmans, London, 1911.

LECKY, W. E. H.: *Democracy and Liberty.* Longmans, London, 1896.

LINGARD, J.: *History of England.* London, 1844.

MCGREGOR, O. R.: *Divorce in England.* Heinemann, London, 1957.

MACQUEEN, John: *A practical treatise on the Appellate Jurisdiction of the House of Lords and Privy Council together with the practice of Parliamentary Divorce.* 1842.

MACQUEEN, John: *The Rights and Liabilities of Husband and Wife.* 1849.

MACQUEEN, John: *A Practical treatise on Divorce and Matrimonial Jurisdiction under the Act of 1857.* 1858.

MACY, Christopher: *Marriage—and Divorce.* Pemberton, London, 1969.

Manchester Guardian.

MASSON, D.: *The Life of John Milton.* London, 1859–1894.

MAYHEW, Henry: *London Labour and the London Poor.* 1851.

MEGARRY, R. E.: *A Manual of the Law of Real Property.* Stevens, London, 1947.

MEGARRY, R. E.: *Miscellany at Law.* Stevens, London, 1955.

MELVILLE, Lewis: *The Duchess of Kingston* (Notable British Trials Series). Wm. Hodge, London, 1927.

MILL, JOHN STUART: *On the Subjection of Women.* 1869.

MILTON, John: *The Doctrine and Discipline of Divorce.* 1643.

MILTON, John: *Tetrachordon.* 1645.

MILTON, John: *Colasterion—a reply to a nameless answer against the Doctrine of Discipline and Divorce.* 1645.

MILTON, John: *The Judgement of Martin Bucer, concerning Divorce.*

MITCHELL, David: *Women on the Warpath.* Cape, London, 1966.

NORTON, Caroline: *A letter to the Queen on Lord Chancellor Cranworth's Marriage and Divorce Bill.* London, 1855.

NORTON, Caroline: *A Review of the Divorce Bill of 1856*. 1857.

PARRY, E. A.: *The Law and the Woman*. C. A. Pearson, London, 1916.

PASSINGHAM, Bernard: *The Divorce Reform Act 1969*. 1970.

PIKE, E. Royston: *Human Documents of the Victorian Golden Age*. Allen and Unwin, London, 1967.

PIKE, E. Royston: *Human Documents of the Age of the Forsytes*. Allen and Unwin, London, 1969.

POLLARD, Robert S. W.: *The Problem of Divorce*. C. A. Watts, 1958.

POYNTER, Thomas: *A concise view of the doctrine and practice of the Ecclesiastical Courts. . . .* London, 1822.

Putting Asunder—A Divorce Law for Contemporary Society. S.P.C.K., London, 1966.

RAYDEN, W.: *Practice and Law of Divorce*. Butterworth, London. (1st-10th edition 1910–67.)

Registrar General's Statistical Review of England and Wales. H.M.S.O., 1968.

ROYAL COMMISSION AND REPORTS OF DEPARTMENTAL COMMITTEES

Lord Campbell	1850–1853 (and evidence).
Lord Gorell	1909–1912 (and evidence).
Lord Denning	1946–1947.
Lord Morton	1951–1955 (and evidence).
Mr. Justice Latey	1967.
Lord Beeching	1969.

RUSSELL, Bertrand, and others: *Divorce as I see it*. 1930.

RUSSELL, Bertrand: *Marriage and Morals*. Allen and Unwin, London, 1929.

RUSSELL, Bertrand: *Autobiography Vol. II*. Allen and Unwin, London, 1968.

SHAW, George Bernard: *Getting Married*. Constable, London, 1908.

SHELFORD, L.: *A Practical Treatise of the Law of Marriage and Divorce and Registration*. London, 1841.

SIMON, Sir Jocelyn: Presidential address to Holdsworth Club *With all my Worldly Goods . . .* 1964.

SIMON, Sir Jocelyn: Address to Law Society Conference *The Seven Pillars of Divorce Reform*. 1965.

SIMON, Sir Jocelyn: Riddell Lecture *Recent Developments in the Matrimonial Law*. 1970.

Solicitors' Journal.

Spectator.

TAYLOR, A. J. P.: *English History 1914–1945.* Oxford University Press, 1965.

THICKNESSE, Ralph: *The Rights and Wrongs of Women.* London, 1909.

The Times.

WALLIS, J. H.: *Someone to turn to—a description of the remedial work of the National Marriage Guidance Council.* 1958.

WILLIAMS, Glanville L.: *The Reform of the Law.* Gollancz, London, 1951.

WOLLSTONECRAFT, Mary: *A Vindication of the Rights of Woman.* 1792.

WOLSELEY, Sir Charles: *The Case of Divorce and Remarriage thereupon discussed, occasioned by the Act of Parliament for divorce of Lord Rosse.* London, 1673.

WOODHAM-SMITH, Cecil: *Florence Nightingale.* Constable, London, 1950.

WOODWARD, E. L.: *The Age of Reform, 1815–1870.* Oxford University Press, 1938.

YOUNG, G. M.: *Victorian England. Portrait of an age.* Oxford University Press, 1936.

YOUNG, RUTH: *The Life of an Educational Worker—Henrietta Busk.* 1934.

INDEX

Abdication Crisis (1936), 107–8, 171, 179

Abse, Leo, 135, 150–2, 161

Access to children, 30–1, 55–7

Addison, Mrs., obtains Private Act of Parliament (1801), 26

Adultery, 26, 42, 43, 73; and Matrimonial Causes Act (1857), 34–6, 38, 42–3; collusion, 87–9; condonation, 89; connivance, 86–7; discretion of the Court, 81–5, 97, 106; 'hotel cases', 77–9; incestuous adultery, 26, 27; legal meaning, 76–7; position from 1923 to 1937, 75, 76; proof of adultery, 77–81

Affidavit of Means, 28

Affinity, law of, 6–8, 10, 12, 26

Agar Ellis, Re, (1883), 55

Alexandra, Queen, 174

Alimony, 27; *see also* Maintenance

Allegation of Faculties, 28–9

Aristotle, 172

Baldwin, Stanley, 108

Barnes, Sir Gorell, *see* Gorell, First Lord

Beaux Stratagem, The (Farquhar), 152

Betoun, Janet, case of, 7

Birkenhead, Lord, 20

Birth rate, 41, 70

Bishop, Edward, 61

Blunt v. *Blunt*, [1943], 83

Boswell's *Life of Johnson*, 25–6

Bowen, Lord Justice, 55

Breakdown of marriage, doctrine of, 114–16, 147–8, 150–1

Brister v. *Brister*, [1970], 111

Britain in the Sixties—The Family and Marriage (Fletcher), 145

Brougham, Henry, 19, 21–2, 27,

59–60, on married women's property, 59–60

Buckmaster, Lord, 75

Bull v. *Bull*, [1968], 83–4

Burke, Edmund, 15

Burnet, Bishop Gilbert, 18

Campbell, Bruce, 87

Campbell, Lord, 62; Chairman of 1850 Royal Commission, 34; on 1857 Act and its effects, 36–7, 39

Care and upbringing of children, 123–5; removal from the country, 131–3

Caroline, Queen, 19

Charles II, King, 39; and Lord Roos's Bill, 17–19

Children, position of, 51–6, 123–5

Church, the, *see* Western Church

Citizens Advice Bureaux, 120

Coke, Lord, 7–8

Collinson, 87–9, 130; and reconciliation, 133–6; changes in law (1963), 89, 125–8, 135–6; definitions, 87–8

Community of Property, principle of, 61, 112

Condonation, 89, 159; and reconciliation, 133–6; change in law (1963), 84; definition, 136

Connivance, 86–7, 158

Consanguinity, 6, 9, 12

Consistory Courts, 9, 23, 28

Contraceptives, 173, 177

Coote, H. C., 28

Cost of divorce, 24, 119

Cottenham, Lord, 55

County Courts; Judges appointed Commissioners, 142; undefended cases transferred to them, 2, 142–3

© Cassell & Co. Ltd. 1971

194